I've been sketchnoting for quite a few years and I thought I knew all I needed to know about visual notetaking. Not so! In her book *Visual Impact*, Wendi Pillars combines *text and visuals* to describe the power of using text and visuals to "connect, clarify, and deepen understanding." Part text, part visual explainer, part tutorial, and ALL reference. This is a comprehensive reference on visual notetaking that illustrates (literally!) the many possible applications of this powerful notetaking and communication method. This book is perfect for the beginner as well as the experienced practitioner. An unexpected bonus of Wendi's approach is that she offers many ways for *you* to show *others* the benefits of visual thinking and describes how you can bring others along on the visual thinking/communication path. I am glad to add this book to my library of references.

— **Rob Dimeo**, Physicist and inveterate doodler

Visual Impact will inspire you and let you into a new understanding of visuals. Wendi shares her gifts with us and lets us in on how and why to use visuals ourselves and with learners of all abilities. I absolutely love referring back to the pages in this book!

— **Valentina Gonzalez**, @ValentinaESL Author and Consultant

Visual Impact!

Published by Wisdom House Books, Inc.
Chapel Hill, North Carolina 27516 USA
1.919.883.4669 | www.wisdomhousebooks.com

Wisdom House Books is committed to excellence in the publishing industry.

Book design copyright © 2021 by Wisdom House Books, Inc. All rights reserved.

Cover and Interior Design by Ted Ruybal

Published in the United States of America

Paperback ISBN: 978-1-7361248-0-2
LCCN: 2021900428

EDU029000 | EDUCATION / Teaching Methods & Materials / General
BUS007010 | BUSINESS & ECONOMICS / Business Communication / Meetings & Presentations
DES007000 | DESIGN / Graphic Arts / General

First Edition

25 24 23 22 21 20 / 10 9 8 7 6 5 4 3 2 1

Visual Impact!

Transform Communication in Your Boardroom, Classroom, or Living Room

Wendi Pillars

Published by Wisdom House Books

Dedication

POPS, YOU, TOO.
YOU'RE ALWAYS
WITH ME. ♡

WITH SO MUCH
LOVE & GRATITUDE, MOM,
FOR ALL YOU'VE DONE
TO ENCOURAGE & TEACH
ME. THANK YOU. ♡

OHIO

NORTH CAROLINA

AND, PSST... IAN, THANKS FOR
ALL the HUGS ALONG the WAY.
YOU'RE ALRIGHT for a 14-YEAR OLD.

Visual Impact: A - Z

Introduction

This is not a "how-to draw" book. As much as I'd love to tell you how to represent x,y, and z with a visual, it's not for me to assume I know what that might look like in your classroom or setting with your particular audience. Sure, there are common symbols or icons that can be foundational in visual notetaking and you'll see some of those later, as well as other ideas to jumpstart your thinking of what is possible. Your work will be to make meaning for yourself with go-to icons for your content and help students as they do the same.

This is book is designed as more of a reference book, something to flip through for boardroom or classroom inspiration, to refer back to, or even to print out the sketches for mini posters. You'll find one page of text followed by a sketch that models what corresponding visual notes can look like, both complementing and supplementing the text. Leaf through the book to analyze my sketches, to see what you feel works and what doesn't, what you notice, what you would either do differently or mirror, and how you might conduct a "think aloud" with this format for your learners as they analyze their own work.

My hope is that you feel empowered along this journey. I'll show you that you have both the tools and the means to accomplish the delightful hat trick of learning: engagement, relevance, and application—while enhancing both the encoding (the memory-stashing part) and recall aspects of learning using visual thinking. Just be willing to give it a shot.

And hey, definitely give *your* version of these sketches a go. My sketches are there as an idea, a jumping off point, a spark. Find your own style and be attentive to your thinking as you create. Have the courage to share via social media, in your classes, or with colleagues and remember to NEVER compare yourself to another or their work. PERIOD. *Comparisonitis* is deadly to your creative soul and can stilt your personal experimentation and style. We don't have time for that. Learning and clear communication await!

Let your inner style shine through, just as you would ask of your audience.

Remember, when you Sketch More, you Think More.

#visualnotes   #visualthinking   #visualcommunication

#sketch   #SketchMore   #ThinkMore

#visualimpact

Introduction to Visual Thinking & Visual Notes

We will start with visual notes, but keep in mind they are a representation of visual thinking and visual communication. They are a combination of words and "nonlinguistic representations", aka, images. They are a form of notetaking that makes the most of synthesizing, chunking ideas, decision-making, connecting ideas, hierarchy, and more to improve understanding. They can be used by all ages, in all content areas, in and out of the classroom, with very little equipment or super high-tech savviness. They generate a powerful cognitive push, but also a lot of fun. They can serve as a quick formative assessment or a more dynamic over-the-course-of-time visual, with spontaneous use or more in-depth preparation.

There are no hard and fast rules, no certain way they should "look" or "be", meaning they're ideal for learning about your students or audience both personally and academically. They are the most versatile tool in my toolbox for brain breaks, quick assessments, and holding students accountable for individual thought. They are useful for reviews and previews, for simplifying complex ideas and enhancing simple ideas. Those are just a few of the reasons I've relied on visual notes in my classroom for decades.

I have personally used visual notes with students in all grades K-12 (and adults!), in military and civilian contexts, overseas and stateside, with resources ranging from sticks and dirt to chalkboards, whiteboards, and iPad projections. As a professional graphic recorder and visual facilitator, I have also used visual notes in the business world for several years, both in person and virtually. Regardless of the context or content, even the simplest of visuals serves as a vehicle for shared understanding, drilling down to the essence of what you want your audience to walk away knowing, and a focal point for clarifying information.

I believe . . .

1. . . . that visual notes are flexible and adaptable to most any situation or context where information is being communicated. A quick sketch, even on my hand or in the dirt can clarify a word or idea quickly.

2. . . . that no one needs to be an artist for visual notes to work their magic; the benefits of simple stick figures and icons far outweigh highly detailed and "perfect" drawings when you're focused on learning.

3. . . . that visuals help transcend language boundaries and participation fears. The confidence learners build transfer to real-world usage, too; not sure how to say something or need to give clear directions? We all know a quick sketch can save the day.

4. . . . that they provide unparalleled, on-the-spot insights into understanding. I can literally "see" what people are thinking in just a couple of minutes which gives me the ability to tweak my instruction or presentation on the spot.

5. . . . that harvesting ideas from others allows people to see that their ideas are being heard and love to see their thoughts captured in a tangible manner.

6. . . . that creating visuals allows learners to sit with information longer, exploring content from myriad perspectives and to make much needed connections among facts and ideas.

BONUS Reason: Using them adds laughter and boosts confidence to take risks both intellectually and creatively, all of which is ideal for building community and ensuring understanding.

For me, visual notes have always been about the thinking process, the actual making sense of material. I constantly wonder: "What can I do, how can I leverage this tool of visual notetaking to help flip my audience's mental switches to a mighty "oh yeah!"? "Which points in the lesson, presentation, and/or content will be the most powerful to stop and synthesize visually?"

I am not saying that using them is easy; in fact, it's often a demanding intellectual push as your audience learns to listen and explore information visually, experiment, revise, and revisit their notes. Add in the analysis of others' notes, with comparison and contrast, justifying one interpretation vs another, and you've got yourself an entire range of rigorous thinking, sparked with even the simplest of visuals.

Reactions will vary: some will exclaim that "this is too hard!" OR "now this makes sense to me" while at other times there will be deep silence as learners allow their brains to shape and express their understandings in new ways.

Visual thinkers are not passive learners. By design, they are taking in knowledge, sorting, categorizing, and chunking it to make meaning for themselves or someone else. Scaffold as needed and try the sketching the content yourself so you can anticipate any struggles as you provide opportunities for visual communication. Chances are the non-passivity of learning will be very new for many. Be patient.

Every mark on a page is a decision, with your participants sifting through not only all things content-related but also concerns about drawing abilities, audience, and purpose. I'll show you how to alleviate those concerns. Just know that visual notes are so much more than "drawing pictures" since they are designed to communicate information. Visual thinking is just like doing workouts for your brain, and the skills required can all improve with practice and training.

Let's get started. Thanks for being here.

- Wendi

Your Objectives

Before you read this book, think about your own objectives for learning. What do you hope to learn? What do you hope to do with visual notes in your organization, classroom, or learning context?

First define why you are here, why YOU are interested in taking visual notes. What do you want to achieve? What do you plan to do with your notes when you create them? Once you set your goals, you'll understand better why you want your audience to take visual notes and how they can use them. As we know, having end goals is the best way to figure out which skills we need to build along the way!

During reading, think about your objectives for your audience's learning. What is the purpose for taking notes or using them? Will they be created for personal use, for hashing out a problem and solution together? Will learners have time to revise them or is this a one-shot deal? Are they going to create tiny margin sketches or larger, more detailed ones? Will they be in a notebook, be hung in the hallway, or tweeted out to the world? Audience and purpose are important.

Determine which concepts of your content are particularly challenging and which are considered non-negotiable "gotta know" information. Which relationships can be highlighted in your content? What knowledge needs to spiral through each unit? Which polysemous (those tricky multiple meaning words!) words beg to be clarified for your content? These are just a few questions to think about before using visual notes.

Not every class or topic lends itself to visual notetaking in the same way, so think about recurring and foundational concepts including vocabulary, audience receptivity and needs, and how you can optimize this strategy as you gain confidence. Remember that ultimately, you want your audience to make and build connections as they categorize and chunk bits of information, discover patterns and trends, then clarify and deepen understanding through different lenses. (It's not just about drawing pictures!)

your objectives

QUESTIONS TO DRIVE & CLARIFY YOUR USE OF VISUAL NOTES:

WHICH CONCEPTS ARE ESPECIALLY CHALLENGING?

WHICH ASPECTS OF YOUR CONTENT ARE CONSIDERED FOUNDATIONAL KNOWLEDGE?

WHICH POLYSEMOUS WORDS BEG TO BE CLARIFIED FOR YOUR CONTEXT? (i.e. "table" in math vs. science vs. civics vs. furniture)

WHICH RELATIONSHIPS CAN BE HIGHLIGHTED IN YOUR CONTENT?

WHICH CONTENT INFORMATION CONTINUES TO SURFACE?

★ NOT EVERY CLASS OR CONTENT LENDS ITSELF TO VISUAL NOTETAKING.

★ CONSIDER RECURRING & FOUNDATIONAL CONCEPTS, INCLUDING VOCABULARY

⋮ CONNECT
⋮ CLARIFY
⋮ DEEPEN UNDERSTANDING

WENDI PILLARS @Wendi322

Why Visual Notes?

This introverted person could chatter on **for hours** talking about why visual notes have been a mainstay in my classroom for **decades!** Yes, for more than twenty years, in classes of all ages, from kindergartners through twelfth graders as well as adults in both civilian and military contexts, both overseas and stateside, in multiple content areas. I've also used them in business settings, helping facilitate meetings and capturing thoughts that are then used to anchor decision-making processes and help everyone recall what transpired.

They're a go-to for me because minimal equipment is needed, visuals transcend language boundaries in tremendous ways, and in my experience, they have served as a connecter of not only ideas but also people.

Visual notes push thinking in ways that other activities don't; they ensure our audience is not passive, holding them tangibly accountable for ideas. No more excuses for mentally tapping out or for letting those two or three learners answer all of your questions!

Visual notes created together become a shared reference for groups and classes, and pull out the essence of conversations and lessons, which in turn help clarify misconceptions. They're engaging to revisit and build upon which is the point of taking notes in the first place. Knowing that they'll be revisited encourages creativity and promotes even more connections as understanding deepens.

Simply put, they make thinking truly visible: when you sketch more, you think more.

This book is designed to spark your imagination using both imagery and words; you will walk away with a slew of ideas about ways to create and use visual notes as a better business communicator, an educator, an explorer of life, and lifelong learner. Here you'll be able to see what you like and what you think could have been done better, tweaking ideas for your own context, objectives, and style. One of the most frequent requests at my workshops has been to "see" how I take notes, or to get copies of handouts created in visual note style.

This book is my response to those requests. Note how I select the text and ideas from one page and sketch it out on the following page; what do you notice about your own thinking as you consider how the information is laid out? What is missing? Think, wonder, learn, and be constructively critical. That's what the powers of visual notes are supposed to provoke. Add to the sketches, sketch below and in margins, and experiment abundantly. Not that you need it, but the permission is all yours!

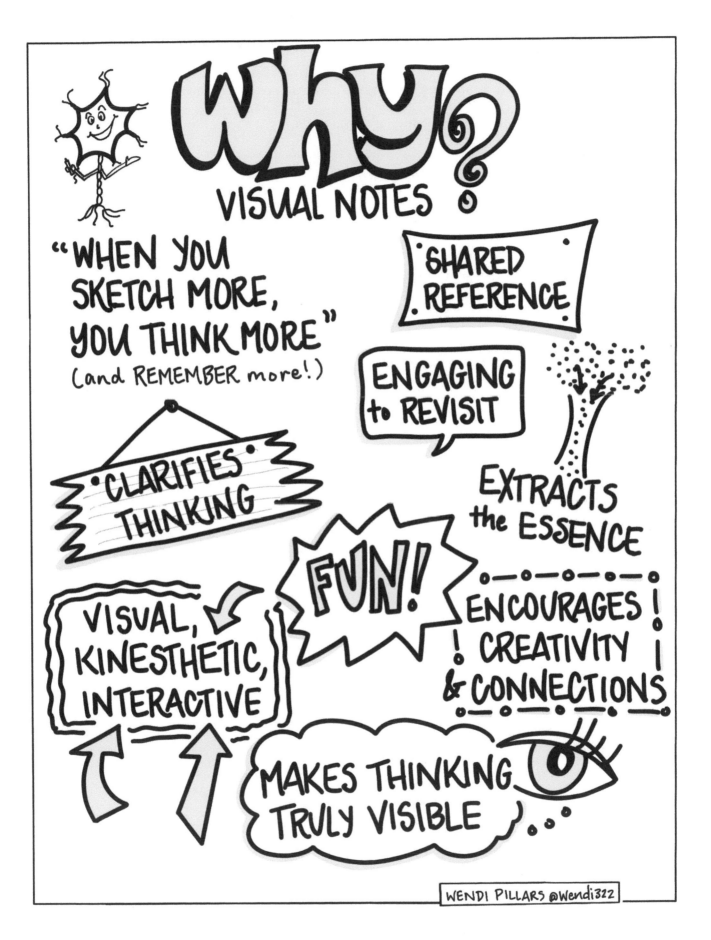

Quick-Start Reminders

Three ideas to keep in mind as you embark on this journey involve materials, mindset, and mastery.

1. Keep your materials simple. The beauty of visual notes is that you can access deeper thinking with just a pen and some paper.

2. Model openness. Demonstrate and model a willingness to try something new or view learning from a different angle. Even adding small sketches and elements will make your work more engaging for learners and will encourage them to try new things themselves.

3. Be gracious with yourself. Mastery is in the eye of the beholder when you are focused on learning and connecting. How is it working for you? Is your work moving you and your learners closer to your objectives? If so, you're on the right track. As you'll see, this style of notetaking is truly about the thinking process.

QUICK-START reminders:

MATERIALS

SOMETHING TO WRITE ON
and SOMETHING TO WRITE WITH

> ✱ One of my FAVORITE aspects of using visual notes is the ACCESSIBILITY FACTOR. Even the simplest tools (sketching with sticks in the dirt!) can help learners make meaning.

MINDSET

"YES! YOU CAN!"

- TRY ONE OR TWO ELEMENTS AT A TIME
- ADD A CONTAINER FOR YOUR TITLE

- REPRESENT ONE MAIN IDEA WITH A VISUAL

REPRESENT ONE OR TWO DETAILS WITH A VISUAL

... and keep expanding!

MASTERY

- ✱ PROGRESS IS YOUR OWN; IT IS A PROCESS
- ✱ SELF-DOUBT IS NORMAL; EXPECT CONFIDENCE TO EBB & FLOW
- ✱ RECOGNIZE PATTERNS FOR YOUR STYLE
- ✱ TRYING IS BETTER THAN DOING NOTHING
- ✱ HAVE A REFERENCE POINT FOR YOUR GROWTH

WENDI PILLARS @Wendi322

Arrows

Arrows, also known as a type of connector, can be used to denote a flow of ideas and hierarchy among ideas through arrow size and shape. They can assist viewers in making connections more explicit by indicating relationships among ideas and providing direction and flow for both sight and thinking. Arrow shapes help align and connect content, enhance it, and point out key ideas to help organize knowledge on the page, and they may be drawn as you sift through texts and information or afterward as you realize more nuanced relationships within your information.

Arrows are also ideal for indicating cause and effect, relationships among facts in a timeline or flowchart, and for pulling together ideas within the drawing.

Using solid lines vs dotted or dashed lines can further show levels of decisiveness. Try solid lines to represent more absolutes and dotted or dashed lines to show that something might be uncertain, a possibility or wish, something in the future, or yet unfinished. Line weight or thickness can also connote hierarchy of ideas; thicker lines equate to main ideas while thinner lines indicate details and larger arrows can contain words and images inside.

Create a code with your learners. Maybe arrow appearance indicates speed—thicker for fast growth, thinner for slower growth, increases or decreases, cycles, or causes and effects. Embolden your learners to communicate and decide as they add a simple layer of complexity and problem-solving into the mix.

Arrows can easily be straight lines that make your drawing more cohesive by directing the viewer in certain directions. Remember that your ultimate goal is to make a collection of notes easier for yourself and others to understand.

WENDI PILLARS @Wendi322

Big Ideas

Sometimes seeing a completed visual note like this can be visually overwhelming, but let's hope it's not the case for this one. This synthesizes for me what I consider to be the 5 Big Ideas of visual notetaking.

You can read it for yourself, so I won't explain it to you (we will touch on all of these throughout the book), but I do want you to notice the layout. How could you do something like this with your students? Could they extract and compile "5 big ideas" (or 3, or 6, etc.) from your class during a single lesson? Over the course of a unit?

Perhaps you could provide the five main ideas (for example), and they sketch the details. Or vice versa. Or perhaps you provide a mix of the two.

Another idea is to create larger unit charts with a handful of big ideas on each one, then post them around the room in sequence, kind of like a timeline. They then become a dynamic teaching tool, one which you can refer back to on a continuous basis as students learn new topics. Have you ever watched your students during a test look to a space on the wall where a poster or word wall used to hang? That association can be powerful for memory recall, cued by the location not only of, say, the poster or visual, but by the organization on the poster itself. Remembering can be influenced by these invisible routines, so I encourage you to rethink how you use your wall space, whether in the classroom or meeting rooms.

Yet one more idea could be to provide your audience with a completed visual note similar in style to this layout about an upcoming unit or lesson, or a challenge that needs to be solved. It can be visually overwhelming for some to do this, so know your learners. Once it is in view, either via document camera, by computer, or individually, break it down by simply asking learners what they notice. Give them time to explore the information and make preliminary sense of it. What do you notice? What do you think we will be learning about? Why is it important? What questions does the visual prompt for you?

What aspects of this sort of template do you envision working for your area of expertise?

What roadblocks might pop up and what is one step you can take to alleviate them?

BIG 5 Ideas

VISUAL NOTETAKING for THINKERS
by WENDI PILLARS
@WENDI322

---

③ VISUALS ARE DOWNRIGHT POWERFUL.

- words as pictures:!
  - icons
  - symbols
  - metaphors
  - idioms, etc.
- transcend barriers

55% HIGHER RECALL just by adding a visual ★

◁ cross-modal connections

VISUALS ↑ LEARNING →

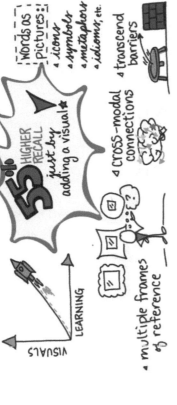

- multiple frames of reference

---

④ YOU HAVE THE SKILLS and the RESOURCES.

- all subjects
  - science
  - math
  - social studies
- Be Bold
- vs

- your space
- incremental progress

★ materials

- languages
- summarize, predict, etc.

◁ new knowledge and old

★ THINKING ABILITY

★ drawing mojo

---

⑤ CELEBRATE YOUR PROGRESS.

your sketches · "their" sketches
★ Do not compare!

🐢 HOW IS your learning?

PROGRESS

---

① IT'S NOT ABOUT ART!

- Synthesize and summarize
- words and images combined

---

② IT MAKES YOUR BRAIN HAPPY.

☆ = more connections
= more learning
= better retrieval
= greater retention

I WANT TO WORK!

★ 86 billion neurons want to transmit & receive info. Let 'em work!

Borders

Borders are another multipurpose visual basic that can be used for emphasis. Some call these containers or frames, but I've always used the word "border" in my classes. (Use the term that works for you!) Regardless of what you call them, they are forms that go around your words, phrases, and ideas to emphasize them, connect them, and embellish them just a bit so they don't disappear into what might be a mass of clustered words. They can be any shape, especially if they enhance the meaning of your work, and they can frame an entire page or a single word or image.

They're very useful for reassuring those who aren't confident in their drawing ability.

Learning to adorn their words with some of these simple frames can increase self-assurance and lead to more courageous visual notetaking. These can be seamlessly inserted into other notetaking formats including Cornell notes. Note: write the text FIRST then draw around it!

Some easy hacks include using lighter shades of the same color, different line thicknesses, dashed lines, dotted lines, or shading. You may even realize you harbor certain subconscious meanings for different shapes, impacting what you feel is most appropriate for a given topic.

Intriguingly, the Bouba/Kiki[1] effect is an experiment that's been around for nearly a century (originally known as the baluba/takete effect) and demonstrates a penchant for associating softer shapes with "bouba" or "baluba" and sharper shapes with "kiki" or "takete." As you craft your visuals, you may find that harder-hitting, more energetic, or more powerful ideas require the added oomph of sharper edges, whereas feelings, possibilities, and reflections may "fit" better with softer shapes. Pay attention to your thinking as you both create and view visuals.

Reflect on your work. Are the borders consistent, with one or two distinctions to set apart information? What stands out for emphasis? What looks out of place? Reflect on why that is and whether it aligns with your goals. A good rule of thumb is to step back and look at your work from a distance or different perspective. Now what do you notice?

Ideas for use include:

- Key words, phrases, ideas
- Provocative and intriguing ideas and events
- Reflections, thoughts
- Foreshadowing, predictions

- Powerful quotes
- Headings and subheadings
- Note classification, categorization
- Evidence for specific purposes, . . . and so much more.

Bullets

Pretty simple visual element, this one.

Basically, bullets can help organize material by chunking content together. Have a bunch of facts? Pull them together by using the same bullets.

Bullets can have a shape or design that aligns directly with the topic, serving as its highlighter. Learning about plants? Use simple leaf shapes to connect ideas. Technology? A simple phone or Wi-Fi icon will do the trick.

Don't forget that you can also use levity to brainstorm your bullet ideas—please, please remember to have fun with this, because if you do, your audience will, too.

Bullets can also help with information retrieval by working as a rapid association tool—i.e., if I see a plant leaf, I know this information relates to plants, whereas a stick figure tells me this relates to people. Which in turn leads to the concept of a shared language within the group or classroom. If everyone relies on a plant leaf for plant-related information, it makes learning and remembering that much easier. Your audience can use agreed-upon common bullets as they take notes, or go back in later and connect facts as a content refresher.

*Note: any type of sketching "code" will help learners worry less about what to draw in the beginning. Collectively determining which icons best represent ideas are a surprisingly meaty class discussion topic that doubles as a formative assessment. Try it! Ask students to come up with ten to fifteen icons for a given assignment or text, and justify why they chose them. You'll be pleasantly surprised!

Bullets

MAKE CONNECTIONS/ CHUNK CONTENT
with like symbols/icons

RAPID ASSOCIATIONS

HIGHLIGHT/ EMPHASIZE TOPIC

What visuals represent your content?

Technology

Food

EMOTION & LEVITY ☺

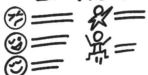

SHARED LANGUAGE

Checklists

I'm not sure about you, but the more time goes by, the harder it is for me to remember all of the things I need to be doing. In order to counter this, I create checklists each day so that I know precisely what I've accomplished and what remains to do because my list typically exceeds my working memory!

We know that chunking information is one way to hold more in our mind by grouping numbers, names, or facts together to make it easier information easier to recall. Of course, that recall also depends on the complexity of the material we're trying to remember and our own level of familiarity with the topic or content. But what is something else that's super easy to do to help?

What you may be finding is that your audience gets stuck after you provide instructions. Why is that? Chances are it has to do with working memory, or short-term memory. There's only so much cognitive space for initial bits of information to be processed and if it's not manipulated or used in some way it is quickly forgotten. Those who speak other languages or come from different cultures may have even more trouble remembering actions that require multiple steps because they are also translating ideas and information.

We can alleviate the anxiety that comes with trying to remember everything by using a simple visual checklist. It may or may not incorporate icons for new or misunderstood vocabulary. Anxiety around not understanding or remembering what is being asked of us can debilitate the learning process; having a place for our internal thoughts to land externally reduces that mental swirl of "all the things." You don't have to worry about what you're forgetting and can instead prioritize or otherwise focus on making progress one action at a time.

Use a checklist as a scaffold, or support, as your audience learns a new process, a new routine, or steps to write a lab report or implement a new initiative. Once learners have learned the routine(s), they don't need the checklist anymore.

Use a checklist to encourage self-assessment. Checking each to-do item off the list promotes reflection on what needs to be done, which order might make the most sense (the variables are in black and white in front of them, so it's easier to see everything at once), and provides a dopamine surge thanks to incremental success each time an item is checked off.

Use a checklist for refinement. Is there something complex that needs to be done? How can you reflect on the process you're using to accomplish that mission and make a better system? Have you ever considered the number of variables we inherently expect others to know or do? Allowing learners to focus on content versus remembering so many steps is a gift.

As far as the visual piece, using icons within the checklist for my learners reinforces new vocabulary and helps encode both the linguistic information as well as the subject matter. Importantly, the checklist itself serves as a visual, too—something that helps with learning because it lessens the cognitive load in working memory and allows learners to focus on the content. It also serves as a reflective means to trigger recall and memory along the way.

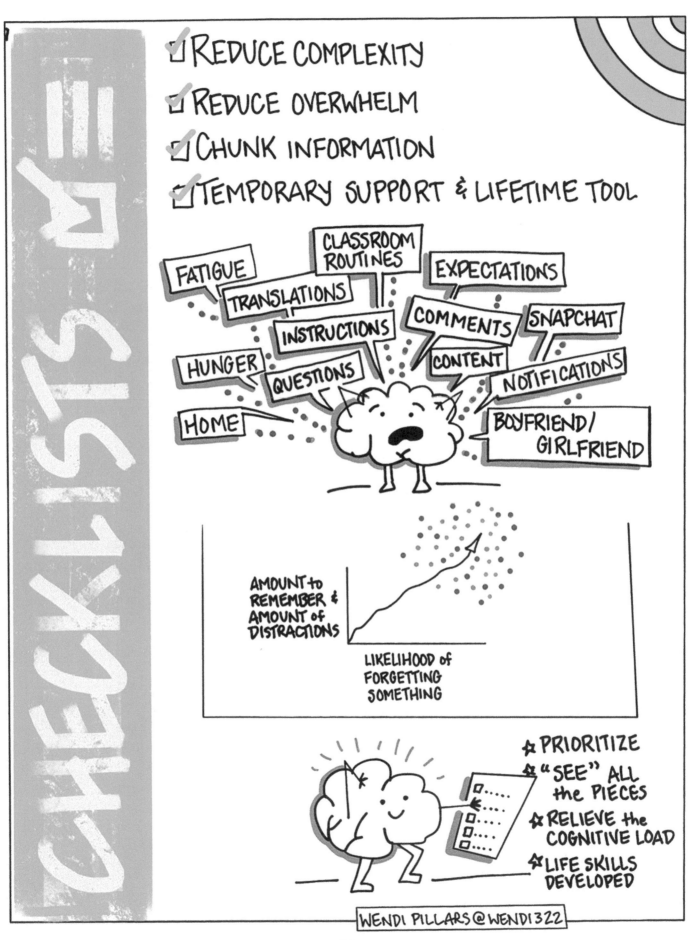

CHECKLISTS

- ✓ REDUCE COMPLEXITY
- ✓ REDUCE OVERWHELM
- ✓ CHUNK INFORMATION
- ✓ TEMPORARY SUPPORT & LIFETIME TOOL

FATIGUE

CLASSROOM ROUTINES

TRANSLATIONS

EXPECTATIONS

INSTRUCTIONS

COMMENTS

SNAPCHAT

HUNGER

QUESTIONS

CONTENT

NOTIFICATIONS

HOME

BOYFRIEND/ GIRLFRIEND

AMOUNT to REMEMBER & AMOUNT of DISTRACTIONS

LIKELIHOOD of FORGETTING SOMETHING

- ✭ PRIORITIZE
- ✭ "SEE" ALL the PIECES
- ✭ RELIEVE the COGNITIVE LOAD
- ✭ LIFE SKILLS DEVELOPED

WENDI PILLARS @WENDI322

—21—

Chunking

How you see and store information will differ from the way anyone else does, regardless of how you received it. Visual notes effectively demonstrate that we can all receive the exact same input, yet our resulting outputs can be vastly different thanks to our own previous experiences and understandings.

One learning strategy we can help our brains optimize is chunking. Using physical "chunks" or bite-size pieces of information and key phrases, we provide our brains with multiple channels to deposit information. If we combine chunks of text with imagery and color, that paves the way for at least three pathways of encoding. The more channels we use to get information in, the more channels from which we can access it and retrieve it when we most need it.

Notice, too, that chunking actually looks like chunks of text. Visual notes don't use long sentences across the page; instead, they rely on phrases and key words that are in short visual bites, maybe two to four words across with multiple lines.

As you can see on the following page, visual notes don't need to be elaborate. Take written facts like the ones on top of the page and turn them into something more visually dynamic. Students will be able to remember placement on the page, color, and visual icons associated with given facts. Synthesizing longer bits of information into chunks is a challenging but transferable skill that is beneficial in all contexts. They can take it further by linking and connecting, extending the visual as they learn more, and clarifying with detail as they go. Asking learners to continually synthesize illuminates gaps in understanding in the moment far better than asking that dangerously vague question: "Does everyone understand?" as we drone through another PowerPoint.

A happy brain is one whose wholeness and myriad skills are being optimized. Brains WANT to work, and they grow by being challenged. Provide those channels to make learning memorable and retrievable.

When you look at the information on the following page, what do you notice? What stands out to you, and how might you use this strategy with your learners?

- Vision is the most dominant sense because it takes up half the human brain's resources. (Medina, 2008)
- The pictorial superiority effect causes humans to remember pictures more easily than words. (Zadina, 2014)
- People remember about 65% of the information presented visually when tested 72 hours after exposure. (Medina, 2008)
- 75% of the human sensory capacity is dedicated to vision.
- Over 90% of information transmitted to the brain is visual.

← SAME INFORMATION ↘

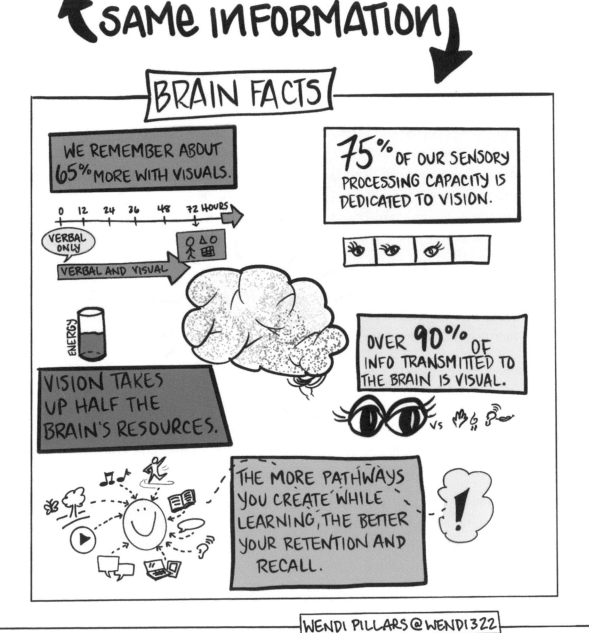

BRAIN FACTS

WE REMEMBER ABOUT 65% MORE WITH VISUALS.

0 12 24 36 48 72 HOURS

VERBAL ONLY

VERBAL AND VISUAL

ENERGY

VISION TAKES UP HALF THE BRAIN'S RESOURCES.

75% OF OUR SENSORY PROCESSING CAPACITY IS DEDICATED TO VISION.

OVER 90% OF INFO TRANSMITTED TO THE BRAIN IS VISUAL.

VS

THE MORE PATHWAYS YOU CREATE WHILE LEARNING, THE BETTER YOUR RETENTION AND RECALL.

!

WENDI PILLARS @WENDI322

Color

I love color, but I've learned the hard way that supplying an array of color (you know, those classroom sets of Crayola markers) for sketching assignments can rouse a bit of excitement, even in high schoolers and adults. The caveat with lots of choice is that having so many colors shifts the focus from content to "art." Students worry far more about making it pretty than getting the content down which adds to the already immense task of notetaking decision-making.

Simple solution: Provide three to four colors max: one or two dark colors and one or two highlight colors to help connect information and make it pop. Teach learners how to optimize the chisel markers with their thick lines, their mid-thickness lines, and the thin lines using the tip of the markers. Even with a single color, hierarchy and handwriting can help ideas pop.

Talk visibility. Darker colors pop, lighter ones are really hard to see, especially from any sort of distance. Three or four colors max help contrast ideas, link others together, and break up any visual monotony without being overwhelming, while minimizing distraction from the content. Remember that every mark is a decision—optimize thinking for content first.

Color can also be used later as part of a review or revision. Visual notes are ideal for revisits, far more so than I've experienced and seen with regular notes. Colors can be used for emphasis, to make additional connections, to categorize ideas and facts or vocabulary words, or to set up questions for further research. They can be an explicit class norm type of "code" for reviewing notes or adding more notes or an agreed-upon formula. If a visual note combines information from two texts, one color could represent one text, a second color could represent the other. Colors could represent teams or note creators. Use your imagination!

Another tip: if you have access to sticky notes, use their color to your advantage. Sketches on pink sticky notes may relate to specific questions while sketches on yellow sticky notes represent vocabulary words. Sticky notes can mirror highlighter colors within the text, too. You get the idea. Make it work for you.

But what about pencil, you ask?

I'm not against pencil, but I encourage marker and pen because I want students to own their work, get over the urge to fix every tiny "mistake," and be resourceful with their marks—how can they fix it creatively? You know your audience, so ask yourself how committed you can encourage them to be, then push them a little bit further.

Remember your role in visual notetaking is to walk the talk and truly focus on how the information they've included supports the topic at hand. Remarks on the aesthetics will negate the powers of visual notes so comment on their use of color as it relates to organization, categorization, and highlighting, for example. With practice, their workstyle will evolve, and that in itself is something to celebrate.

COLOR

EVERY MARK IS A DECISION: OPTIMIZE THINKING for CONTENT FIRST. wp

TIP: (non-scientific)

3-4 COLORS MAX

TRY COLORED STICKY NOTES

MARKER = commitment

no erasers!
mistakes are OK!

ONE or TWO DARK COLORS
- main ideas
- titles
- subheadings
- Key vocab

ONE or TWO HIGHLIGHT COLORS
- details
- containers, frames
- highlight shadows
- bullets
- specific words/phrases
- contrast
- connect

REVIEW TOOL:
☆ encourage revision using color-oriented activities
- underline vocabulary
- new connections
- draw containers around newly relevant details

CLASSROOM CONVERSATION
☆ discuss & create color "code"

▨ vocab	☐ text 1	☐ surprising connection(s)
☐ main ideas	☐ text 2	

☆ discuss new connections, which details to prioritize, words to revisit and emphasize

WENDI PILLARS @WENDI322

Community

When people study information, a challenge, or a process through a visual lens, it jumpstarts a transformative knowledge dive as a community. Not only does it help drill down to the essence, or core, of the challenge or information, but it also provides clarity to build it back up and out.

Once the core is clearly laid out, it's easier to unearth logical gaps in understanding. It lessens forgetting and sparks understanding, making it easier to organize and manipulate moving parts into useful chunks and sequences. It becomes a conceptual anchor to support group processes.

Using visual notes begins with an active intention to get and keep people engaged consistently. Start with small, do-able steps or tasks. Invite other's input, whether verbally or visually, and provide plenty of markers for everyone to draw and scribe. Intriguingly, when a sketch is the focal and landing point for your group, whether with adults or kids, energy is directed toward addressing the sketch rather than aiming any criticism at a person. Participants feel more comfortable diving into a problem or clarifying a roadmap when everyone sees the same referent material. Such comfort impacts how people participate as well as how they perceive and retain facts amid information overflow.

This kind of engagement moves participants to stand and work together, away from the safety of their chairs and phones in their laps. We need to model and encourage these changes. You'll be surprised how simple movement into a different space can foster community while extracting you as the leader from sole responsibility for feedback or driving the conversation.

As a community leader in a business or educational setting or beyond, what do you want to spend your time together doing? Do you want to talk at your audience, or would you rather learn what they are thinking, what they understand, and how to move forward together while leveraging others' emotional and intellectual energy? Whose input do you currently give value to? What might change if your meetings included co-created visuals? What would "more engagement" really look like to you? What would change if everyone were truly "present"?

Critically, how do "better communication skills" manifest themselves in your context? I've heard many goals around this phrase, yet very few deliverables address it. Visual thinking is one powerful way to achieve that, especially since drawing out ideas also forces us to slow down and actually listen to each other. Drawing together naturally forces us to clarify in an authentic way because we ask our increasingly supportive community questions like: *"Is this what you meant?,"* *"Do you mean this should go here/ there?,"* *"What else do we need/ what are we missing here?,"* or *"How can we represent this better with a visual?"*

Imagine, then draw your way through business re-opening plans post-COVID-19, with heated emotion, polarized views, AND a visual focal point to help neutralize them. Your community with its knowledge-sharing and feedback provision will become self-supporting and more sustainable without you having to do all the prompting and responding. Encourage it.

Constraints

Remember in art class when you were given a blank piece of paper and told to draw something, and your brain just froze? I do. It still happens now—someone will ask me to "draw something" and I freeze. I'm not a person who draws for the sake of drawing, and I have definite challenges when it comes to drawing a scene from my imagination.

However, if someone told me to sketch something specific, my paralysis would thaw, and I could sketch out the needed imagery. The point is this: if your audience knows the expectations, they may still be anxious about drawing but at least the anxiety about "what to draw" will be alleviated. Constraints are about the mental as much as the physical drawing process; what we perceive as our limits vs what may be a plateau, lack of confidence, or simple lack of experience. Constraints can also be couched in expectations of purpose, time limits, and audience to help guide visual thinkers as they learn to take notes.

Along with providing a purpose for sketching, limit drawing space. Fold paper into quadrants, into sixths, into three columns—whatever matches your objectives and goals the best. Having a limited space makes it far less daunting, grants a tiny shot of courage, and also helps keep the visual notetaking to a stricter time limit. Kids tend to only use a small amount of space if you give them an entire piece of paper anyway. Make it meaningful. Sticky notes work well for this and have the added bonus of being movable or shareable, not quite as permanent.

Index cards are another great sketching canvas. Details can be added on the back and they can be sorted, categorized, sequenced, traded, and more. They can be stored with a rubber band, in a bag, or on a ring, keeping them readily accessible. Simple icons or symbols in the upper corners of the cards or a colored line around the edges of the card can help categorize them. No need for fancy tools, but you can certainly ramp up the utility of what you have.

One important note about smaller spaces. Rather than an invitation to cram as much as you can into them, you can also challenge learners to be pithy, to be increasingly concise. How simply can they convey what they know? This can have quite an effect on their thinking, far more integrative than listing "everything" they do know during a review session, or for planning next steps, for example. Constraints spark creativity. Pay attention.

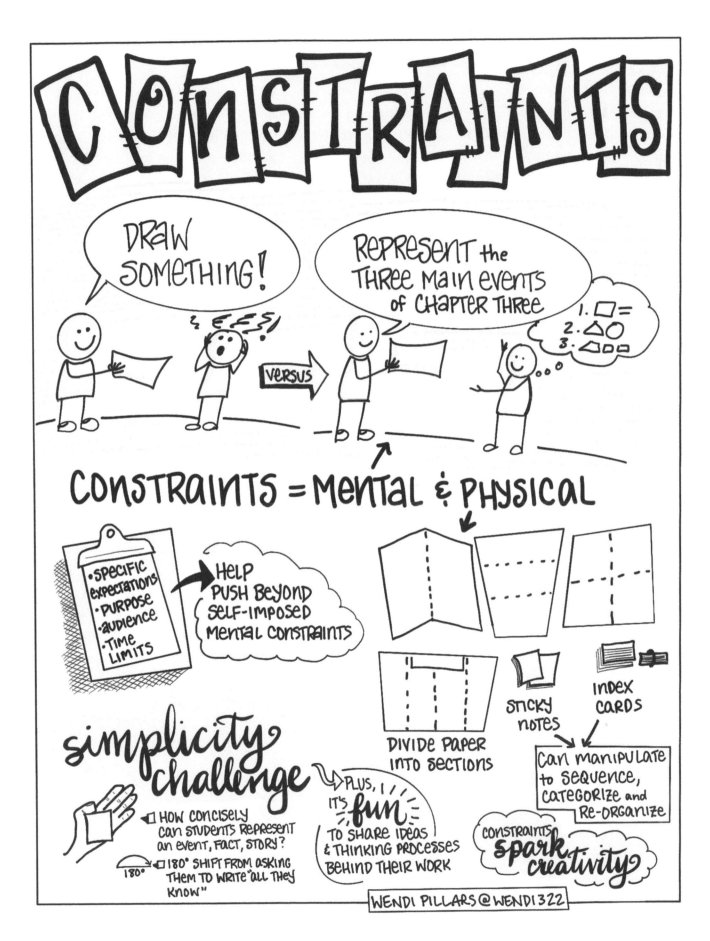

Culturally Responsive Teaching,
Part 1: Introduction

One noticeable takeaway from my years of using visuals is how quickly we can default to what we know and what we are comfortable with. Sometimes in sketching, we are aiming for rapid representations, moving and thinking quickly just to get an image down to help us remember better. Which is good. Listening is hard; synthesizing on the fly is really hard. These skills are incredibly valuable for life.

Sometimes, though, we are working with a more tenuous topic, something more sensitive or one in which the content has a distinct tone, origin, and nuance. This is where our next steps thinking-wise come in.

In order to hold conflicting ideas in tandem, to record ideas from a perspective that honors all voices present physically or within text, we have internal work to do. As we consider how to represent ideas, we also want to consider what kind of image might be a stereotype, which images generalize a culture or perhaps completely disregard its values. There's no way to capture every single nuance or cultural reference. Instead what I'm saying is that we want to use the tool of visual notes, the strategy of visual notetaking, to dig just a little deeper into our conversations, to use them as a tool to help clarify "what I really mean is . . . ."

We want to both support and challenge our learners every step of the way, and through visual notes, we can maintain high expectations while questioning how our own culture and experiences shape who we are. We can see it in the way others "hear" things others don't, or visualize the same words in an array of thought-provoking sketches. As we sketch, we talk about how what we hear, what we note, and what we draw enhances or mitigates discriminatory practices. Why it matters. What we can do differently.

Zaretta B. Hammond[1] states that "culture guides how we process information" (p.48), and that plays out in our classrooms and organizations if only we look for it. I remember working in my first high school overseas where nearly all of my students "cheated" outright on tests. In frustration, I asked colleagues what to do and they looked at me with surprise saying, "Oh, yes, they 'help' each other all the time." While it was strikingly different from what I was used to, it became a pivot point in how my view of the world informed what I did and how I reacted in my classroom. Do your students and colleagues operate from individualistic or communal views? Is there a powerful oral tradition with front-porch sitting and storytelling or a bent towards reading stories? I may write every day in my home, but I also know that so many of my students may or may not even have a pen or pencil to write with, or have never seen their parents write. It is our responsibility to become more aware of these differences and to grasp them as opportunities for tailoring our expectations and how we communicate them with each other.

I'm far more mindful about this aspect of my practice because of my work with multicultural organizations and my learners who keep it real for me. It took me years to begin to consider these questions, but I encourage you to start having these conversations with your colleagues, team members, or students now. They often have ideas and answers that are beautifully realistic and honest, highlighting yet another aspect of culturally responsive teaching—a genuine respect and appreciation for each person's uniqueness and cultural ways of knowing.

CULTURALLY RESPONSIVE *teaching*

ASSETS-BASED PERSPECTIVE:

✻ Consider and value diverse languages, backgrounds, and experiences as powerful foundations for learning.

LEARNING IS STUDENT-CENTERED:

Choice

Goal-setting

Clear objectives

Relationship-building

Modeling

Student grouping

Opportunities to share about their lives

Ability to contribute meaningfully

SUPPORT & CHALLENGE STUDENTS:

Maintain high expectations

Scaffold as needed and as appropriate

KEEP IN MIND:

- WHO has power
- WHO has privilege
- HOW are they enhancing and/or mitigating discriminatory practices

⭐ HOW DOES YOUR OWN CULTURE SHAPE WHO YOU ARE AS A PERSON? EDUCATOR? IN TURN, HOW DOES THAT SHAPE YOUR EXPECTATIONS FOR OTHERS?

WENDI PILLARS @ WENDI322

Culturally Responsive Teaching,
Part 2: Listening & Receiving Information

When I mention visual notetaking or people see me recording with graphics, the focus is always on the "art" of it. The outcome, if you will.

What is often forgotten or even dismissed is the act of listening while sketching and creating said "art". Throughout this book I've referred to the myriad processes and activities occurring in our brains as we sketch, sift, decide, interpret, write and draw, and these create a useful analogy for culturally responsive teaching and presenting.

Imagine for just a moment, what would happen if we entered our conference arenas, zoom meetings, and classrooms with the primary intentions of listening and receiving information. Visual note takers work from this angle. We are not there to constantly give, give, give information without input from our audiences. Instead, we listen for the in-between spaces, for what's *not* being said, and by whom.

Visual thinkers make conscious decisions about what to include—or not-–in a sketch, based upon not only our ability level or speed, but also our background knowledge, awareness of the speaker's objectives, and the audience itself. Teaching others how to listen is necessary. There is a tremendous difference between bearing witness visually and judging speaker content. We, in the words of Oscar Trimboli, have power over what we pay attention to vs what we give attention to. Where are your attentions?

These are all important considerations for each presentation we give, each class we teach, each person we encounter. How are we honoring each other's stories through our listening and recording? What is the ratio of our listening to talking? What should that ratio be?

Through listening, we become equipped to ask better questions. We become more culturally conscious, a term I first learned from Gloria Ladson-Billings, which means we become more aware of what we see and how that might differ from what and who others see, levels of access, and what systems are in place. Those experiences form powerful background knowledge which in turn impacts how we show up on any given day. Although we may not share similar experiences, the act of listening can help lessen the understanding and empathy gaps.

Listening more and more closely gives us tools to find cultural touchpoints, to determine whose perspectives are missing or written off, and to help us teach both what is familiar and what is unfamiliar. In other words, it helps us build our community, whatever form that takes.

In a room (virtual or face to face) full of thinkers with deeply individual understandings, being able to co-create a one-page summary of thoughts, processes, and/or ideas is a massive triumph of improved communication that has room and permission to evolve.

I challenge you to listen more, eventually listening as much as you talk. How might that look? How can you capture interpretations visually? What is one step you can take toward that 50/50 ratio? What can you do 1% differently today? How can visuals help you tell today's story?

CULTURALLY RESPONSIVE
listening & receiving

BECOME a LISTENER, a "WITNESS", NOT JUST an ARTIST—

☆ LISTEN for the *in-between* spaces
☆ WHAT'S *not* BEING SAID?

☆ MAKE CONSCIOUS DECISIONS ABOUT WHAT to INCLUDE —OR NOT— in a SKETCH

BIAS

☆ *witness* vs. *judge* of INFO PRESENTED

"*paying* ATTENTION to —versus— *giving* ATTENTION to"

OSCARTRIMBOLI.COM

50/50?
— LISTENING vs. TALKING —
WHAT'S *your* RATIO? WHAT *should* IT BE?

Dividers

A simple way to organize notes is by using dividers. These can be used handily within scholarly Cornell notes (as pictured) and as part of any other visual notetaking page. They can be scaled up to run across a page, between paragraphs or around an entire page, or scaled down to separate smaller learning bits. These are another "gateway visual," something easy enough to draw to entice learners to consider their content in new ways and to chunk it for better understanding and utility.

In need of inspiration? An internet search for bullet journals will fill you with ideas on different styles.

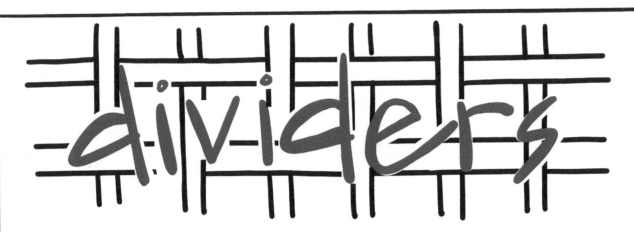

dividers

cornell notes

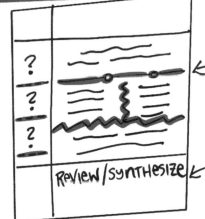

Review/synthesize

"CHUNK" INFORMATION

SET IT APART

use DIVIDERS IN ESTABLISHED NOTETAKING ROUTINES

INCORPORATE VISUAL SUMMARIES, TOO

style? anything goes!

- solid ———————
- dashed - - - - - -
- dotted · · · · · · · ·
- filled ▬▬▬▬▬
- shapes △——△——
- icons —👤—👍—
- decorative 〰〰〰

- imaginative

Drawing

I know this isn't a "how-to-draw" book but here are a few useful tips to help your thinking pop on the page without too much extra work. Rely on basic shapes to start with. Have fun, embellish them, and combine them together. Use basic drop shadows, too: simple gray lines or contrast lines around part of a shape can add quick dimension to your work.

The biggest resistance to doing this kind of work is the mindset of "not being able to draw." We ALL can draw a stick figure and basic shapes. We can combine them, and we can practice. Yes, it takes practice, but I'm just going to tell you that you can. Moving on.

Finding inspiration: Move, stretch, go for a walk, step outside, get some water, read something unrelated to the topic because you never know what will inspire a fresh outlook. If all of that fails, then try a Google search with the words "icon" or "clip art" for simpler imagery, or explore The Noun Project[2]. There are plenty of stock images, so my suggestion is to have at least a kernel of an idea in mind and aim to enhance it with ideas you find. Oh, and in class, always ask students or team members how *they* would represent a concept...then hand them the marker! Others have solid, creative ideas, and seeds that you can expand into something more.

Copying images: I'm asked all the time about copying images, and a gripe I have is students' immediate penchant to trace an image directly on their computer screen. I do support them in taking inspiration from pictures but push them to make it their own. I also talk about how normal it can be to not have ideas and reiterate that thinking and sifting through thoughts is a continual process! This also highlights the value of having a visual library for quick access to ready mental images, even basic icons, and boosting confidence through preparation.

As for image use, remember to follow these steps when you conduct a Google image search:

Click on image→   Tools→   Usage Rights→   Labelled for reuse (or reuse with modification).

This ensures you are within your rights to, as Austin Kleon says, "Steal like an artist" and make it better with your own flair.

Copying from me: I often start out by encouraging learners to follow along with me when I'm sketching. Doing this shows that sketching is routine and expected. Grumbling may ensue, but carry on. Whether creating visual notes as a review, notes during a lesson, or talking through a sequence of events, it's a golden opportunity for a think aloud about both content and my sketching process. I might focus on how to organize the notes, how much to write vs draw, patterns that I see emerging, visual elements (bullets, borders) that help pull together connections, lettering hierarchy, or emphasis on particular words and ideas. Focus on one or two elements when starting out and check in frequently with your learners. Simple = perfect as long as the information is accurate. You'll figure out quickly who needs support to copy and who is prepared to explode with their own creativity.

Above all else, you must remember this is about progress and process. Perfection is never the goal. Learning always is.

DRAWING

BASIC SHAPES

+

DROP SHADOWS

LIGHT SOURCE

$\square$ + L = $\square$

$\triangle$ + ∠ = $\triangle$

+

"MENTAL GLUE" to COMBINE BASIC SHAPES

$\square$ + + ○○○ =

$\square$ + = NOTES

○ + △ + ? =

○ + ||| + | =

○ + △▽ + O + |||| =

△ + ▷ =

finding inspiration

LOOK AROUND YOU!
'M' = LOGOS   SIGNS

COLOR PALETTES

the ENVIRONMENT

• LOOK SLOWLY
• CONSIDER DIFFERENT ANGLES

WENDI PILLARS @WENDI322

The Drawing Effect

I've heard more times than I can remember that "drawing pictures" isn't beneficial, useful, practical, or even appropriate, especially when done with older learners. I am obviously passionate about the fact that they carry all of the benefits above, no matter the age of my students, from grades k-12 to adults, businesses worldwide and even military personnel. If clearer communication is the goal, then drawing out ideas deserves a chance.

A 2014 study[3] called "The Drawing Effect: Evidence for reliable and robust memory benefits in free recall" aimed to answer whether drawing improves thinking and memory better than simply writing notes. The study was comprised of seven experiments with individuals and groups of people assigned to draw pictures to represent lists of thirty words or to simply copy the words repeatedly for a certain amount of time. Artistic talent was irrelevant, and—spoiler alert—drawn words were recalled later at a higher rate in all seven experiments.

It didn't matter if participants listed semantic characteristics of the words (parts of the word, part of speech, root words, contextual meaning, etc.), viewed pictures of an object on the list, or simply visualized a mental picture of a given word. The individuals and groups experienced higher recall when drawing the objects on the lists. They remember more, which means they are more equipped to apply and act upon what they know.

What this means is that our learners will likely benefit from the visual thinking behind the drawing effect—both in the moment and later when reviewing or studying. We've all read about how elite athletes visualize their every move in a game or practice for better success; we can take that one step further with our audience and have them visualize themselves being successful AND what others' reactions are to their success. Sketching this out leads to much greater clarity and lower anxiety.

One other (anecdotal and non-scientific, but firsthand) result of incorporating more drawing with others is that a palpable lightening of the room occurs. It's beneficial for a mental respite on one hand while serving as a cognitive push on the other. Learners relax, chatter quietly, laugh, and compare ideas when given time to draw. Why wouldn't we want these myriad benefits in our boardrooms or classrooms?

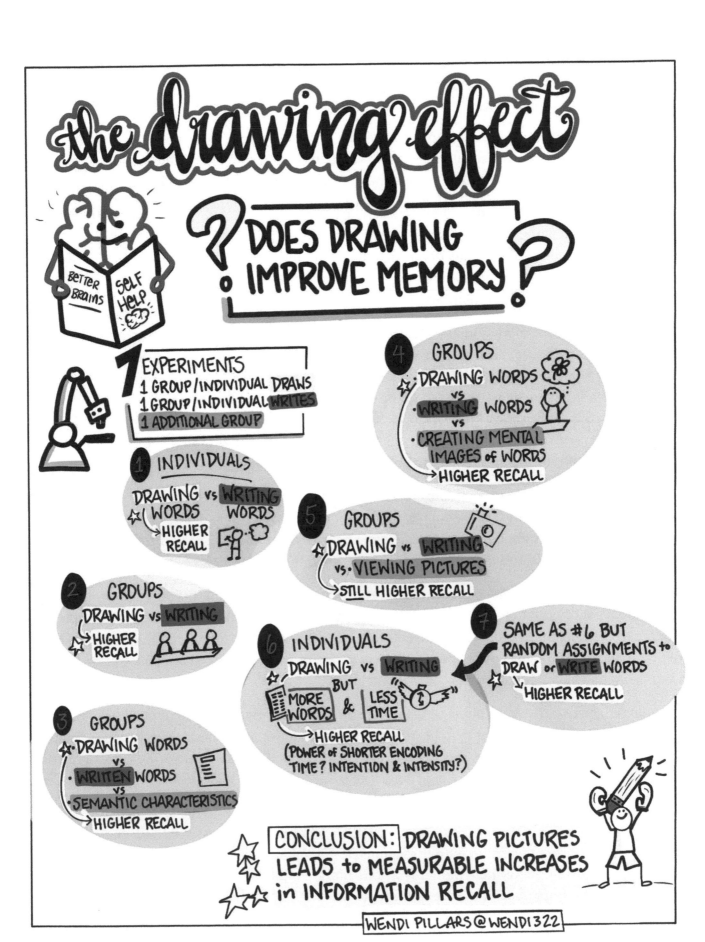

the **drawing effect**

? DOES DRAWING IMPROVE MEMORY ?

7 EXPERIMENTS
- 1 GROUP/INDIVIDUAL DRAWS
- 1 GROUP/INDIVIDUAL WRITES
- 1 ADDITIONAL GROUP

1 INDIVIDUALS
DRAWING vs WRITING WORDS → HIGHER RECALL

2 GROUPS
DRAWING vs WRITING → HIGHER RECALL

3 GROUPS
- DRAWING WORDS
  vs
- WRITTEN WORDS
  vs
- SEMANTIC CHARACTERISTICS
  → HIGHER RECALL

4 GROUPS
- DRAWING WORDS
  vs
- WRITING WORDS
  vs
- CREATING MENTAL IMAGES of WORDS
  → HIGHER RECALL

5 GROUPS
DRAWING vs WRITING vs VIEWING PICTURES → STILL HIGHER RECALL

6 INDIVIDUALS
DRAWING vs WRITING BUT MORE WORDS & LESS TIME → HIGHER RECALL
(POWER of SHORTER ENCODING TIME? INTENTION & INTENSITY?)

7 SAME AS #6 BUT RANDOM ASSIGNMENTS to DRAW or WRITE WORDS → HIGHER RECALL

CONCLUSION: DRAWING PICTURES LEADS to MEASURABLE INCREASES in INFORMATION RECALL

WENDI PILLARS @WENDI322

—39—

Dynamic Visuals,
Part 1: Introduction

Let's say your students create a one-page visual note rife with tidbits for formative assessment. Maybe they go on to use them for review or for a follow-up written or oral presentation . . . sounds great but let's take a page from scientific modeling and make student visuals even more dynamic.

We know that drawing something out rather than just thinking about it vaults a person's thinking out of theory and into tangibility. Once you can see it, then you can play with it, develop it, discover areas of personal expertise and unanswered questions. Imagine a scientist in the field who makes a plan, anticipates findings, adds details to corroborate their hypothesis, and returns home to craft a fabulous write-up of all the confirmations of their predictions. Easy, right?

Except that's not how it works. Instead, scientists are more likely to encounter obstacles, counter-evidence to their hypotheses, and gaps in understanding that end up raising even more questions. Back to the drawing board they go, sketching out revisions, additions, and removals from their initial model. This type of scientific modeling, included in the Next Generation Science Standards, doesn't require a 3D model but does use 2D sketches. This type of sketch is revisited over time to track learning, find gaps, map out experiments, and design hypotheses. It is a "living document" rather than a one-time sketch, created with the purpose of revising and revisiting over the course of a unit or lesson.

Creating an initial model about a topic brings numerous questions to the surface. How do I begin? What should I include? What should I leave out (for now or for good)? What ideas are missing? What information do I need to make this more complete/ make more sense? What imagery makes this more understandable? What are the visible and invisible factors impacting this issue? Which perspective is key? . . .

Building upon the initial model becomes a mighty cognitive push. As the model evolves, missing links become apparent, thought processes deepen, thinking evolves, and learners realize how complex a simple idea can actually be. The process helps visualize cause and effect, clarify connections, and develop thinking. It boosts confidence over time as learners and team members begin tangibly tracking what they are exploring and experiencing.

Visual thinkers can start from a point of what they already know and are able to observe. Perhaps there are specific expectations for what is to be included, a list of non-negotiables as more detail is added with each learning stage or component. It is not enough to talk about it; both instructors and participants must experience it firsthand. This is a visual way for learners to demonstrate their deepening understanding of a phenomena, make their reasoning available to others, and revise and manipulate their now-visible thinking.

Encourage reflection on both process and content, on what has been learned, how their thinking has shifted over the course of learning with these models, and what they will do differently for the next one. What questions would make their model revisions more complex and nuanced? What surprised them about the process? It will become a transformative shift in your use of modeling; expand learning by making visual notes come alive.

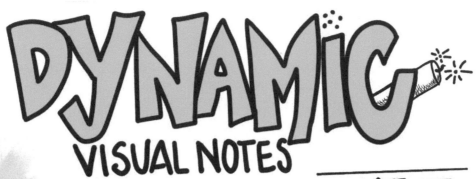

DYNAMIC
VISUAL NOTES

REViSit & MAKE CHANGES
notes
WITH SUBSEQUENT RE-READS

the HOLY GRAIL of NOTE-TAKING

Different colors for emphasis or specific texts

Use colors to connect similar ideas / concepts

Use colors to distinguish between what is added and/or revised

Highlight, underline, or draw borders around sketches that correspond directly with textual evidence

Craft visuals for specific sentences or chunks of text & include all details

Share

Partner sharing, gallery walks, whole group presentations, chat stations, and more, will optimize learning.

BLACK → 1st Resource

GREEN → 2nd Resource

RED → 3rd Resource

↳ Additions/Revisions

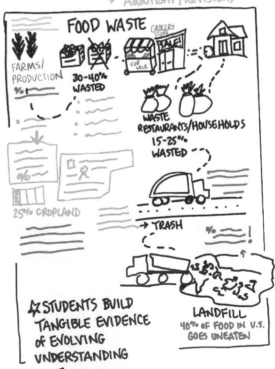

FOOD WASTE

FARMS/ PRODUCTION %

30-40% WASTED

CROCERY STORE

25% CROPLAND

WASTE RESTAURANTS/HOUSEHOLDS 15-25% WASTED

→ TRASH

LANDFILL 40% OF FOOD IN U.S. GOES UNEATEN

☆ STUDENTS BUILD TANGIBLE EVIDENCE of EVOLVING UNDERSTANDING

↳ CAN THEN CREATE FINAL DRAFT INCORPORATING ALL DETAILS.

WENDI PILLARS @ WENDI322

Dynamic Visuals,
Part 2: Home Base for Learning

As aforementioned, using sketches this way has transformed my thinking and expectations around learning as well as how I present a topic or anchoring phenomenon. I wanted to share another look at what one of these models might look like as a home base for learning and you can find student examples in the Appendices.

Think of the visual as a home base, something we keep returning to over the course of a unit, multiple lessons, or stages of a business process. Use an essential question, overarching theme, or similar type of prompt as a driver, OR as the model develops, new questions may arise that beg to be pursued. Ideally, the modeling will become a learning and clarifying tool, not another "poster" which collects information. We want these to be messy, not perfect, with a goal of helping think through an explanation. This type of visual is not a product in and of itself, but rather a catalyst for discovering connections and uncovering both hidden ideas and questions.

In my experience, this type of visual thinking promotes thinking and conversations, with the sketch as a focal point. It's not about getting it "right," but rather the manipulation of the ideas, the molding, the playing with and examining of ideas. The thinking and discussing about what to include in the visual and how to best represent it are where the intellectual efforts kick into high gear. This is also why I lean toward analog sketching, because it's easier for me to see what's going on and there's a larger canvas to invite more voices than a small screen does.

Collaborative efforts in creating a visual model also help level the playing field: those who know the terminology can help others hear it in context, language learners and shy group members can practice discussing ideas before sharing out into larger groups, and group member expertise can be tapped. Time limits can be set if needed, but I find that monitoring engagement is critical. As a facilitator, you can constantly push for more thinking through pointed questioning.

When getting started, think about whether you want learners to start with a blank piece of paper so you can see what emerges and what their background knowledge holds. Alternatively, you can show them a model to kick-start their thinking. It truly depends on your goals and learners. I always have a mix of learners that are ready to work on their own with minimal support and plenty who need more guidance. For those who need even more guidance, or if you'd prefer that the audience's work is somewhat similar, provide a template for them to work on or a list of non-negotiables to include in the sketch that they can use for self-assessment.

As they get started, prompt your thinkers with ideas about what should be included and what can be left out. What is most important and what might be irrelevant? What connections can you make to any of the components or elements in the sketch? What causes those connections? Are they causes or effects? What are the visible elements involved vs the invisible?

I do use these visuals as formative assessments, but rely on reflective evidence-based written responses for grading purposes. Some learners create a more polished final visual because it is helpful for them to define connections more clearly. Combined models and written responses are incredibly insightful, as are the actions that the consequent understandings inspire.

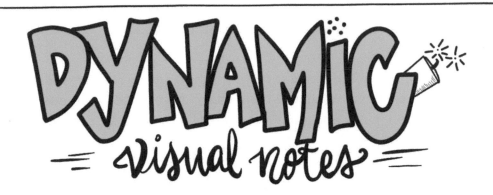

DYNAMIC visual notes

Rather than think of a visual as a one-time collection of information, facts and ideas, consider it a **HOME BASE** for you and your students' learning.

Relate title to **ESSENTIAL QUESTION** or overarching theme

Serves as **ANCHOR / FOCAL POINT** for subsequent information

KEY with list of resources, color-coded

COLOR CODE each text/resource is represented with a new color

TITLE

1 - article
2 - lab report
3 - video

SPACE for questions that arise

VISIBILITY of thinking prompts deeper level of processing

Use **STICKY NOTES** to add information

Teachers and students can readily **TRACK LEARNING** and integrate ideas **TANGIBLY**.

SEEKING CONNECTIONS becomes a "new norm"

"What **RELATIONSHIPS** exist and why do they matter?"

Promotes **RETENTION** & **RECALL** as students continue to deepen connections to previously learned material

WENDI PILLARS @ WENDI322

—43—

Dynamic Visuals,
Part 3: The Model as a Mental Sandbox

When using this format, think of the model as more of a tool to get groups of students to think together or to gauge individual understanding. Use them as an idea sandbox where students can play with ideas. The conversations and debates about what to include on the model and how to best represent it comprise a heavy intellectual lift!

Consider the needs of your students and ways to encourage them to move from pure text to the act of modeling understanding through visuals like these. Decide whether you want students to use a template (to ensure support and some similarity), to see a pre-made model exemplar, or to rely on a blank piece of paper to see what emerges. Each has its own pros and cons, levels of student agency, and levels of support. You'll also need to decide whether you want students to create an individual model first, then share and combine ideas, or to start as a group first.

Templates do provide support but may stifle some creativity or set a different "bar" of learning than you'd prefer. Talk through an initial model together, eliciting ideas together about how the components are connected to each other and why. A simple "before/during/after" template is a solid place to start for providing some structure but not too much.

Teachers increasingly ask about digital formats for this, but—you know me by now—I feel strongly that drawing out ideas, whether as part of a group or individually with opportunities to banter with peers during the process, is critically important. Conversation happens, students can compare with others and ask questions, and it's important for me to see what students are thinking. I do allow students to use the internet or articles as references for finding photos or icons because it's challenging to imagine all that you need to—but, I push students to rely on each other's knowledge and imagination first and foremost. We don't know how extensive a student's background knowledge is and it's okay if they don't know much because there will be more growth on their revised model!

The initial model will be the biggest challenge, especially as you balance your own expertise and back-ground knowledge with what you might expect or even want students to know. It's always a balancing act between the big picture and the details; a minimal amount of detail and knowledge is needed to make the modeling even possible, so plan accordingly. The initial model may need to be a response to an article, to be built up with subsequent information.

As far as a title goes, it's interesting how adding a title constrains thinking, with the model ending up a more "posterized" collection board of ideas. What we really want is something messy and imperfect and a means of helping them think through an explanation. Decide what role you want the model to play in your classroom, because it has powers to push deeper thinking. Consider your assessment needs, too, since the moment we "assess" something it changes its role for us.

My simple take is to use the model as the mental sandbox and written reflections throughout the process for more formal assessments. I'm still working on it, but it's worth the investment of time, and I've used it for more than science. (Check out Model-based inquiry for more ideas.)

DYNAMIC VISUALS: MODEL-BASED

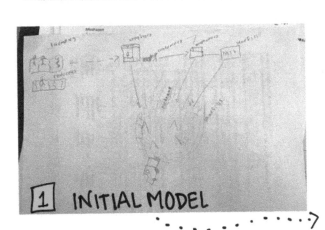

1 INITIAL MODEL

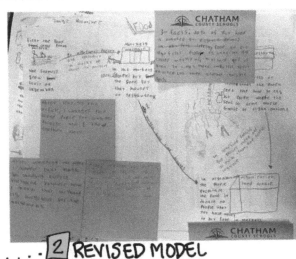

2 REVISED MODEL

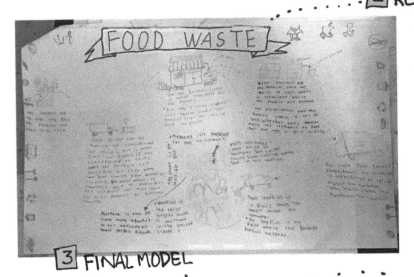

3 FINAL MODEL

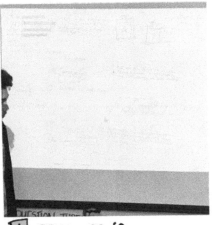

4 PRESENTING SOLUTIONS for CHALLENGES UNCOVERED DURING LEARNING PROCESS.

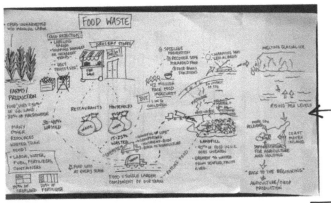

REVISED MODELS CAN USE DIFFERENT COLORS AND STICKY NOTES (#2) TO INDICATE PHASED LEARNING or DIFFERENT SOURCES OF INFO.

WENDI PILLARS @WENDI322

Elements of Art

Okay, a little truth bomb here. This was the last page and visual note I created. I was so hesitant to include this because I truly want the emphasis of visual notes to be on the thinking process. Our brains change every time we learn something new, and that, to me, is astounding. I want that to remain the emphasis with our visual thinkers, too, because it's a powerful reminder that they also have agency in the growth of their thinking.

I've also never been formally trained as an artist and never studied it. I know that others use various elements of art to describe it and value it, but I'm simply going to talk about some elements that do come into play with visual notes. These can be talking points and considerations for anyone to further analyze their own work if they're interested in aesthetics.

Lines are everywhere. Thick, thin, medium sized, curvy, spirals . . . they can make a difference when portraying hierarchy, connections, divisions, or grouping ideas together. They can highlight or set apart ideas, and help control how much space is used.

Shapes can be geometric or organic, and as you'll see throughout the book, I rely heavily upon the basics, both large and small, around a word or two, as the foundation of images, and around entire pages. They can be filled with color or designs or simply empty, separate from other shapes, or connected.

Balance is something my audiences seem to just "pick up on" without me really talking about it. There's a lot of natural understanding revealed in creating notes, especially with kids. They don't worry about it like adults do, and when given the space, they just go at it. Balance for them means spreading out information over the space of a page. For me? That works. It also pushes them to add imagery or facts on the "other side" if they feel there's imbalance.

Proximity relates to balance and is also useful for grouping like ideas and facts.

Progression relates to hierarchy and can be combined with different line thicknesses or main ideas and their details, or main categories and subcategories.

Movement is how the notes draw your eye across the page. From left to right? Top to bottom? Center to the periphery? Where is your story taking me?

Exaggeration for me also relates to hierarchy. Those big ideas, great quotes, and things we don't want to forget are physically bigger on the page, sometimes in extreme ways, for heightened attention and focus.

Contrast can relate to colors, shapes, line thickness, and content ideas, while repetition can be seen in bullet points, color use, shape or imagery similarities, and even word use.

Color and negative space each have their own page in this book.

elements of ART

·FIND YOUR PALETTE·
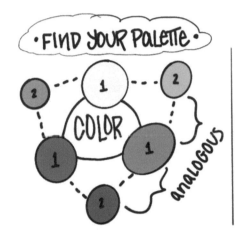
COLOR

analogous

1-PRIMARY COLORS
2-SECONDARY COLORS

LINES

BALANCE

SHAPES
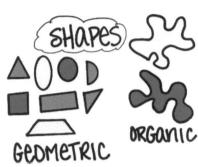
GEOMETRIC   ORGANIC

SPACE
POSITIVE   negative

PROXIMITY

PROGRESSION

MOVEMENT
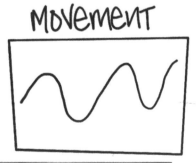

CONTRAST

REPETITION

exaggeration

WENDI PILLARS @ WENDI322

Equity Literacy

Equity issues abound in our schools and businesses, from technology access to communication challenges across language barriers and socioeconomic divides. From support for myriad developmental needs to food insecurity and homelessness issues, leaders have a lot to think about, address, and accommodate.

Far from a panacea, visual notes still come into play thanks to their capacity to reveal what our audiences are really thinking. Every person is infused with background knowledge and schema, that lens through which they process their experiences and knowledge, and we can value all of it by providing space to express oneself through sketches. Fancy isn't necessary when you're asking someone to tell you more, to connect themselves to the content, and most of all—granting the time to do so. Give time to think through information and align it with what they already know in order to honor their stories with words and visuals.

There are also myriad experiences we readily assume others have had, but those assumptions are through our personal lenses, so caution is imperative. Instead of just asking if anyone has ever owned a pet, maybe they could sketch an animal that would make an awful pet. They can be creative, there's no wrong answer if they justify their response, and regardless of their personal experiences with pets, they can still participate fully in the conversation.

A conversation like this, as "silly" as it might seem, opens doors for us as leaders to understand our learners through a personal, assets-based lens while rethinking our biases and limiting assumptions. We can use information from their sketches and discussions about them to anchor our instruction, we can steal ideas from them for future learning hooks, and gradually build stamina for more in-depth thinking routines. And subsequent steps taken will be better informed.

Providing space for people to process and share information through even the simplest of sketches has provided audiences unexpected and compelling insights. For example, many of my students don't have what might be thought of as "basic photos" of their family and home. Talk about a vibe killer when you can't even participate fully in an introductory activity about yourself and your family. Instead, an activity of explaining and narrating a short storyboard of sketches helps ensure everyone is on slightly more even footing. What assumptions are you making about how your team members are equipped to contribute?

Sketching also provides far more depth in responses than if I ask learners to define, predict, or summarize in mere words. In addition to an oral explanation? That's good stuff.

What would happen if you tried the same, even with concepts you "think" your team members and learners already know? What surprises and insights might you encounter?

EQUITY LITERACY

"INTERRUPT CYCLES of OPPRESSION"

FRAMEWORK to ENABLE EDUCATORS to THREATEN the → EXISTENCE of *inequity*

RECOGNIZE HOW **ACCESS & OPPORTUNITY** ARE DISTRIBUTED UNFAIRLY

REDRESS CONDITIONS THAT CREATE INEQUITY

HOW CAN WE HELP STUDENTS LEVERAGE WHAT THEY DO HAVE?

ADVOCATE for ACCESS, RESOURCES, ENGAGEMENT & VISIBILITY

ELEVATE STUDENT VOICE

NOTES:

- BUILD ON STUDENTS' KNOWLEDGE: SKETCHES PROVIDE UNTAPPED INSIGHTS ⇒ VALUE THEIR SCHEMA!
- EVERYONE'S SCHEMA IS PERSONAL & CULTURALLY GROUNDED
- SKETCHING TIME ALLOWS TIME FOR PROCESSING

WENDI PILLARS @WENDI322

Facilitate Discussion,
Part 1: Modeling Curiosity

Walk into my classroom and you might see a student at the whiteboard or using the document camera, asking classmates to tell them more. Facilitating is an act of helping others make clear progress towards, or achieve, a goal. This is something used in business organizations, something that companies clamor for and something we do every single day in our classroom. Using visuals as part of a group process—whether learning or explaining something new, brainstorming, revamping ideas, envisioning, or mapping lessons learned—the visual, the sketch, becomes a shared reference to support everyone's learning.

As a facilitator tangibly drawing out others' thinking and providing a conversational focal point on paper or a whiteboard, you are modeling curiosity (*tell me more about that*); bravery (*I am in front of all of you and I'm not sure how to draw this, but I'm trying*); openness to feedback (*That's not right? Then tell me what I can do to make it right.*); and attention to detail. (*Can you repeat that statement again? I want to make sure I recorded that correctly.*)

Ever see painters at work at a street fair? There's typically a huge crowd around them wondering what the artist will do next as they proceed in their artistic flow. How about an RSA animate video? There is anticipation of the drawing happening within your brain, laced with predictions, wonder, curiosity, reflections, affirmations, and maybe even surprise as you see the imagery come to life. This type of observation is an enticing interplay of neural activity, far from passive learning.

As a facilitator, sketching out conversations and ideas is engaging and therefore more memorable, while the messiness of it invites others to participate more. This back and forth conversation and "listening with a marker" provides real-time assessment and opportunities for active listening and clarity. Ideations are messy processes, ones that can emerge unpredictably, fostering at once a tolerance for not knowing and a desire to get clearer in our thinking.

Facilitating a discussion is not the same as creating one of those huge, striking graphic recordings you might have seen at a conference. Those are a one-shot deal: when the speaker is done, the graphic is complete. Facilitating entails embracing the processes of revising, clarifying, inviting others to participate in the making, while modeling a unique vulnerability as you ensure others are heard and their thinking is acknowledged accurately.

Facilitated discussions are also a great place to co-create some icons related to a project or unit. What are some key words? List them out. *What are some icons we can come up with to represent those key ideas? Can we co-create them together? Okay now, let's put them together and retell the story, your weekend adventure, the process of our experiment, or the steps of our proposed solution. How did our main character or product get from here all the way over there? Let's start at the beginning and you tell me what to write as I visually capture what you know and your concerns.* If eighty-four percent of all people are visual learners, then talking through processes, content, timelines, role expectations, and more will be far more effective than simply "telling" your information. Turn that marker over to someone else. Give them the chance and the confidence to practice questioning, listening, sketching quickly, and being open to criticism. That's a big ask of anyone, so be supportive as they help draw out others' thinking.

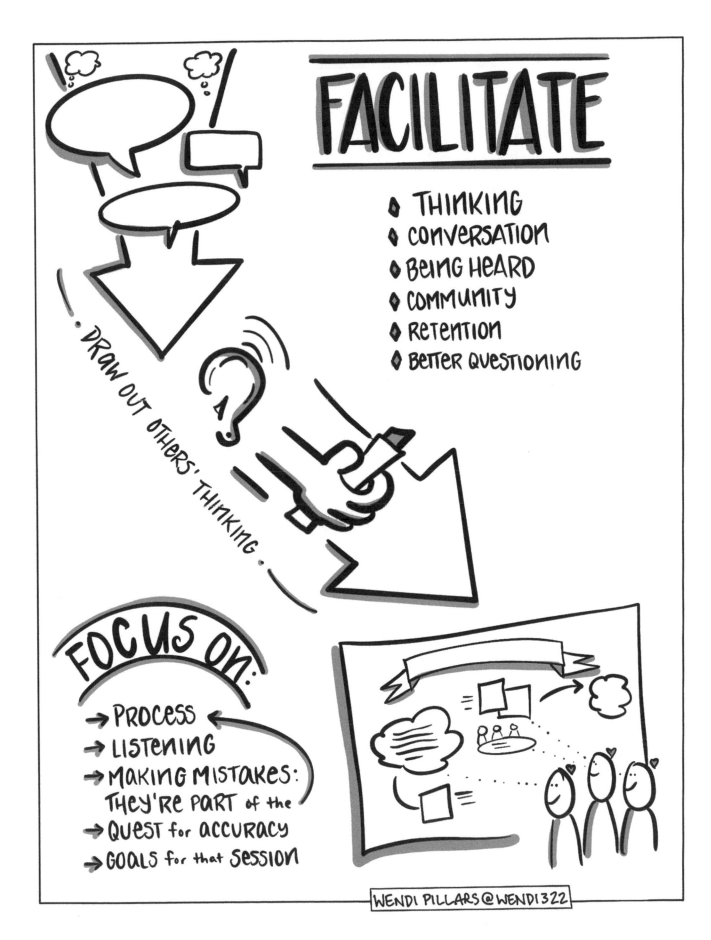

FACILITATE

- THINKING
- CONVERSATION
- BEING HEARD
- COMMUNITY
- RETENTION
- BETTER QUESTIONING

...DRAW OUT OTHERS' THINKING...

FOCUS ON:

- → PROCESS ←
- → LISTENING
- → MAKING MISTAKES: THEY'RE PART of the
- → QUEST for ACCURACY
- → GOALS for that SESSION

Facilitate Discussion,
Part 2: Collaborating & Listening

One of the biggest takeaways from a facilitation mindset is the fact that it works best when we stop talking. When we listen and when we model listening, we encourage learners to participate, to add their voices while we validate what they think and believe.

When we facilitate conversations, we are guiding the learning process, engaging others, and ceding control over the content covered. Higher participation and greater amounts of input are needed for this to work, so it takes time to establish norms, particularly around sharing ideas that differ from others. To facilitate well we listen more than we talk. And we listen with intention to understand, so it behooves us to have good questions, genuine curiosity, and patience on hand for anyone unaccustomed to communicating their ideas.

When ideas differ from what we have in mind try a "yes, and . . ." response to recognize what others are bringing to the table. Modeling this also invites others to share ideas with each other, not only you, and values different realities.

This isn't easy. There's no "hack" to great facilitation and in a sense, we are at once asking for and providing permission for our audiences to become more engaged in thinking than if we fired off rhetorical questions or lectures. We just need to practice. Good questions, ones that can either be answered out loud or serve as prompts for quiet reflection are needed, as well as ones that clarify, push, and lead ideas.

Everyone has something to learn and space to grow. We cannot assume we know what someone knows (or not) and why that is. The point is for us to ensure the time with us is well-spent, engaging, and a model for increasingly effective communication.

FACILITATE

MINDSET SHIFT

MORE ABOUT THE *how* WE COMMUNICATE THAN THE *what* WE ARE TRYING to COMMUNICATE

GREATER PARTICIPANT AGENCY

→ teaching vs. PRESENTING

→ collaborating with vs. FACILITATING

WHAT WILL THIS LOOK LIKE FOR **you**, YOUR CONTEXT & YOUR PURPOSE?

YES, AND...
↳ ENCOURAGES LEARNERS to ADD THEIR VOICES
↳ ACKNOWLEDGES IDEAS
↳ PROVIDES SPACE for POSSIBILITY
↳ VALIDATES THOUGHTS & BELIEFS

GOOD QUESTIONS
○ LEAD to LEARNING
○ NOT ALWAYS SEEKING the "RIGHT" ANSWER
○ DIFFERENT TYPES of QUESTIONS
○ BEST QUESTIONS EVOKE LEARNING

YOUR VOICE is *valued*
YOUR BACKGROUND, EXPERIENCES & IDEAS

↑ CURIOSITY ↑ RESPECT AMONG COMMUNITY

facilitators NEED to STOP TALKING & LET the LEARNERS SHARE WHAT they KNOW & HOW they FEEL

WENDI PILLARS @ WENDI322

—53—

Four Domains of Learning

In the language learning world, there are four primary domains of communication to address: reading, writing, listening, and speaking. Reading and listening are receptive skills, meaning that they are skills that involve understanding words and language—the "input" of language and its nuances. Strategies to enhance these skills include highlighting key ideas and vocabulary, supporting developing understanding of concrete and abstract ideas, using visual supports and graphic organizers or templates.

Speaking and writing are expressive skills, or generative, which means that learners are producing language. We support these skills by taking time, modeling, expanding, and adding information, and using other ways to communicate besides speech, to name a few strategies.

On the following page are just some of the standards that can be addressed using visual notes in your classroom. Providing space for visual thinking and communication can support or enhance learning and meet myriad requirements found in the standards. Even though standards vary by location, many of these are applicable to all content areas and grade levels, in formal and informal settings.

Even in the military, pre-mission briefings and after-action reviews use visual thinking to ensure crystal clear communication about not only information, but also processes, steps and sequences, personnel roles, and reflections. If organizations with lives on the line realize how visual communication helps ensure clarity, how many ways can you incorporate visual thinking to transform your own organization's progress, communication, and thinking?

SPEAKING

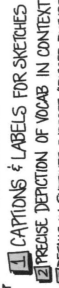

1. EXPLAIN, DESCRIBE, JUSTIFY SKETCHES & SKETCH ELEMENTS
2. RESPOND THOUGHTFULLY TO DIVERSE PERSPECTIVES
3. SUMMARIZE POINTS OF AGREEMENT/DISAGREEMENT
4. CLARIFY, VERIFY OR CHALLENGE OTHERS' IDEAS
5. POSE & RESPOND TO QUESTIONS
6. HAVE STUDENTS DEMONSTRATE THEIR SKETCHING, LETTERING, ETC.
7. COLLABORATE TO VERBALLY SIFT THROUGH IDEAS

WRITING

1. CAPTIONS & LABELS FOR SKETCHES
2. PRECISE DEPICTION OF VOCAB IN CONTEXT
3. DETAILS IN SKETCHES SUPPORT "BIGGER PICTURE", JUST LIKE WRITING
4. SKETCH WORDS, PHRASES, STANZAS, EVENTS, ETC; FIND APPROPRIATE WAY TO "CHUNK" INFO
5. BRAINSTORMING, PRE-WRITING, DURING WRITING, & TO COMPLEMENT WRITING
6. ORGANIZE COMPLEX IDEAS, CLARIFY RELATIONSHIPS AMONG IDEAS
7. CONSIDER AUDIENCE

ETC!...

2-3 MINUTES PER QUICK SKETCH MAX!

USE COMPLETED SKETCHES:
1. SHARED REFERENCE
2. REVISIT, REVIEW
3. COMPARE, CONTRAST
4. EVALUATE EFFECTIVENESS OF VISUALS CREATED

accessing the 4 DOMAINS with VISUAL NOTES

WENDI PILLARS • @WENDI322

just TRY it!

LISTENING

1. LISTENING COMPREHENSION
2. ACTIVE LISTENING → HOW MANY DETAILS?
3. TEACHER PROVIDES DETAILS; STUDENTS SKETCH MAIN IDEA
4. LISTEN TO PART OF SOMETHING & SKETCH WHAT HAPPENS NEXT
5. SKETCH THE SPEAKER
6. BUILD ON OTHERS' IDEAS
7. MAKE NEW CONNECTIONS IN LIGHT OF REASONING & EVIDENCE

READING

1. SKETCH DURING 1st READ OF COMPLEX TEXT USING TITLE, HEADINGS, VOCAB, ETC.
2. COMPREHENSION: SKETCH BY PAGE, STANZA, SECTION, PHRASES, KEY TERMS, ETC.
3. FIGURATIVE LANGUAGE, NUANCES, TONE
4. WORDLESS SUMMARIES
5. REVISIT & MAKE CHANGES WITH SUBSEQUENT RE-READS (USE DIFFERENT COLORS)
6. USE DETAILS OF SKETCH TO CITE THROUGH TEXTUAL EVIDENCE
7. PROVIDE OBJECTIVE SUMMARY OF TEXT

Four Steps to Learning

From a biological standpoint, all learning is about change. James Zull realizes that "if a teacher has any success at all, she has produced physical change in her student's brain. Teaching is the art of changing the brain"[4] in the sense that we are creating conditions that lead to change in a learner's brain, not controlling it or otherwise rearranging it.

I just want to emphasize that again because it is mind-blowing to me: we as educators and leaders have tremendous responsibility because **when our audiences are learning, they are physically changing their brains!** Dr. Judy Willis, a neuroscientist turned middle school science teacher (now *that's* a heck of a combination) calls learning "bloodless brain surgery!" I tell my learners if they learn just one thing, they will go home with an entirely different brain than the one they showed up with this morning.

Learning, in its basic form, tends to consist of four steps:

1. The brain receives some sort of input.

2. The brain reflects, analyzes, and makes necessary connections.

3. The brain cobbles the bits and pieces together, manipulating the information to make meaning.

4. The brain exhorts us to do something with that information, applying it and taking some sort of action to test it out.

Everyone needs opportunities to change their brains, and to do so means opportunities to transform input into output, to receive and **use knowledge,** which is what sketching so naturally promotes.

These steps are not always linear or sequential, and as you know, we can vacillate between reflection and manipulating ideas over and over. We may test things and return to generating more ideas. What this learning cycle does is remind us that it is not enough for our learners and organizational members to have information: they must use the idea and action parts of the brain and **apply what they know.** When this happens, learning and understanding are cemented more readily into long-term memory.

Isn't it remarkable that we as leaders play a role in changing brains every single day?

Wow.

Grading,
Part 1: Assessment Tips, Templates, Rubrics

A las, a perennial question I hear again and again: "How do you 'grade' visual notes?"

Quick answer? I typically use visual notes as a formative assessment, which in turn helps guide my next bit of instruction. If I see learners are zipping right through quick sketches, with nuance, detail, or even humor I know I can move on, maybe even picking up the pace. On the other hand, I can also quickly see what concepts I need to review, explain in a different way, or clarify somehow.

Tips to consider:

Determine whether you want to assess learners' thinking process or their product. Are you looking at how they're pulling together disparate pieces and making connections to prior knowledge? Are you relying on all the little sketches to inform your instruction? Or are you going to wait for them to present a more polished final sketch, for example? Maybe their product is unfinished but will be a conversation and decision-making tool as participants collaborate with peers using their respective sketches to show and build upon their thinking. Imperfect sketches invite participation—how can you use that to your learners' advantage?

Templates can be designed fairly quickly if you know what you want your audience or learners to find as they read, listen, and discuss ideas and information. As a scaffold, it helps keep them on track as they find the essence of lessons, talks, and resources, and it can reduce any artistic anxiety regarding how to organize ideas once they find them. It can restrict some creativity, too, but I always provide the option to sketch out their own on blank paper, as long as accurate and essential information is included. (Find examples in the Appendix).

Rubrics also provide clear expectations for student work as they work through their process, particularly for more in-depth visuals. I do not focus on artistic quality, but I do require that the work be legible and neat if it's a final polished product because others will be viewing it. If it's a more comprehensive process, I'll expect more informational non-negotiables, such as facts and vocabulary that I feel are an absolute minimum. I'll also expect hierarchy in the lettering that shows a difference between the main idea and any details, icons and sketches that make supportive sense. Lastly, I ask for an insightful written reflection on both the process of visual notetaking and a learner's final product or certain iterations. It may be helpful to begin with a checklist of your non-negotiables to keep them on track before using an actual rubric.

For organizations and businesses, grading isn't appropriate, but finding ways to have team members and colleagues reflect on the process, or illuminate their takeaways, will certainly ensure that meetings and professional development sessions are interactive and provide leaders with a live feedback loop.

GRADING: VISUAL NOTES
the perennial question
"HOW DO I ASSESS VISUAL NOTES?"

TEMPLATE

TITLE

MAIN IDEA

VOCAB

ANCHORING

DETAILS

PHENOMENON

CONNECTIONS

+ At-a-glance for completion
+ Ensures key points are addressed
+ Reduces any artistic anxiety regarding organization of ideas
+ Built-in scaffolds to guide ELLs
- Can restrict student creativity (can always allow student choice: blank paper v. template)

RUBRIC

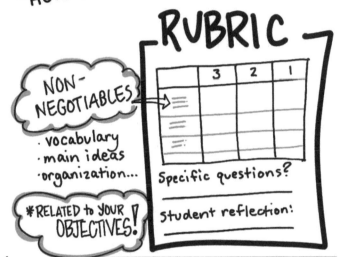

NON-NEGOTIABLES
· vocabulary
· main ideas
· organization...

*RELATED to your OBJECTIVES!

	3	2	1

Specific questions?

Student reflection:

+ Clear expectations for student work; guides process, too
+ Simplifies assessment focus
- May restrict creativity; students may focus on minimum

PROCESS or PRODUCT?

3 R's
∘ reflections throughout
∘ revisions
∘ responsiveness to feedback

sufficient & accurate content

personal interpretation

novelty, humor

organization

valid connections

legibility

artistic aesthetics

WENDI PILLARS @ WENDI 322

Grading,
Part 2: Additional Considerations

As you can probably tell, my idea of "grading" when it comes to the actual visual notes leans largely toward formative assessments. Every once in a while, I'll include responses that require visual notes on summative assessments, but the expectations are very clear, there may be a word bank included, and it will be something similar to what they've already practiced in class.

Considerations for you:

Formative assessment:

- Consider which types of information will best represent content understanding. Graphs? People? Facts? Questions? Diagrams? Storyboard sequence?

- Have an idea of what you want to see in visual notes, including any non-negotiables to demonstrate understanding. Maybe you even have a "what I don't want to see" list.

- Find good stopping points in your lesson or presentation where learners can synthesize. Have questions prepared and on hand for further explanations and oracy practice.

Actual sketching:

- Two to three minutes is PLENTY of time for you to gauge understanding of an entire group, but you must be circulating, looking, and interacting. This is not a time to assign a quick task and sit down.

- Consider whether learners will create small quick margin notes, slightly larger sticky note sketches or index cards, or build upon a larger one over multiple days.

Uses of sketches:

- Visual thinkers can share with the whole group or partners, explain their partner's sketch, share process or content, justify their selection of a particular fact, or even explain how they drew something specific.

- Teach learners how to use sketches as a review tool, building block or support tool for further projects, effective review or during high-stakes scenarios. More often than not, visual notes serve as a springboard for another activity rather than the end-all-be-all.

- Sketches can function as a shared reference from a guest speaker or classroom experience, co-created and then displayed where everyone can view it. They can also be shared with authors or speakers via social media and used in newsletters and thank yous.

Revisit and revise:

- Make time for learners to dip back into their notes throughout a session or lesson and model how the information contained within them can be used to respond to questions or provoke curiosity for further research. Encourage them to seek and identify additional connections using arrows and bullet points or color, for example.

- As always, content understanding, time available and learning objectives should drive final sketch expectations. Why are they creating them? What do they need to walk away knowing today?

GRADING:
part two

FORMATIVE:

What types of information best represent content understanding?

Have an idea of what you want to see in your students' sketches

STOP and **SYNTHESIZE**

"Sassy" POINTS

Where are good stopping points in your lesson?

CREATE:

How much time will you plan on for quick sketches?

★ This is NOT a time to assign work then sit down. <u>Seeing</u> student work is CRUCIAL!

★ 2-3 minutes is PLENTY of time to circulate through the classroom and gauge where everyone's thinking is!

SHARE:

★ Acknowledge student work, effort, thinking

★ ASK students if they are willing to share whole group

★ Students can share work with partners, quads

★ Students can explain <u>their</u> partner's sketch

★ Students can share with the whole class

★ Can share CONTENT or PROCESS

★ Can describe <u>WHY</u> they chose to draw what they did

★ Can explain <u>HOW</u> they drew something specific

REVISE:

★ as determined by understanding, time and overall learning objectives

WENDI PILLARS @ WENDI 322

Handwriting,
Part 1: Legibility

Seems that teaching handwriting has become a controversial subject these days, at least in the United States. Regardless of your beliefs about spending class time to focus expressly on handwriting, let me just whisper that visual notetaking is like stealth handwriting practice. (Shhhhhh! . . .) Whether visual thinkers are using a digital device or analog, they have to make certain that their writing is legible so that their work is useful to themselves or another intended audience.

I know I push content and "process over pretty" incessantly in this book, with better understanding as the supreme grail. Handwriting and lettering are essential, however, and can become a safe entry point into sketching, especially for the more reluctant. Plant seeds by demonstrating how to draw block letters, their name in bubble or graffiti letters, and other fun designs.

Teaching learners informational hierarchy through lettering can be a gamechanger as it supports the rationale of both different styles of writing and different "sizes" of ideas as a student sifts through information. In other words, it's another lens through which to view content and ideas. Larger, bold letters are used for main ideas, titles, big ideas, surprising ideas, or ideas that truly resonate. Smaller, lower case letters are more typically used for details to support and enhance the main ideas. "Fancy" letters of all kinds can be used for fun titles or to evoke a mood.

Varying the width or thickness of handwritten lines is not only an exercise for fine motor skills, but also for varying emphases. You may want to discuss norms around other styles and expectations!

Have students revisit their notes: can they find patterns? How can they differentiate their notes to indicate bigger ideas vs details? What background information do they need to know in order to better distinguish between the two? How could handwriting play a role in formative assessments?

If you're wondering how to fit this into your instruction, integrate it into your presentation hook or warm-ups, or ask that participants write their exit ticket/reflection with different handwriting than they normally do. Have large paper hanging with questions on each for participants to respond to visually. Ask them to write main ideas with thick lines, and three details with a thinner line. Give them paper with wavy lines and ask them to write a quote following the curves. Write words inside of a box or around the edges of a paper. Who knows what will flip a switch? Doing these kinds of activities spurs creativity, provides permission to play, builds confidence, and moves the brain out of a linear pattern of thinking. No excuses, really.

HANDWRITING

HELLO!
sunshine
serifs dots
WELCOME BACK
Outline
IAN '22.
PLANT POTTED
LMÃO
MAKE A WISH
Good Morning
WHY?
NAME
SOUND
Iain FABULOUS!

★LEGIBILITY is IMPORTANT!★

small writing USES→ fingers

normal writing USES→ Wrist

BIGGER! USES→ more arm.

PRACTICE WITH PANGRAMS:
(sentences using all 26 alphabet letters)
☆ The quick brown fox jumps over a lazy dog.
☆ Pack my box with five dozen liquor jugs.

Wet
CReate Mix it up!

WENDI PILLARS @ WENDI 322

Handwriting, Part 2: Tips & Tricks

One of the easiest things I've done to promote lettering and handwriting is to print out the alphabet from Microsoft Word using four or five fonts I think are replicable. Print out both lower and upper case alphabets and all the numbers in a large size (36-48 range, maybe larger for younger learners) so that students can trace, tweak, and experiment. There are increasingly more places online that offer handwriting sheets for practice, especially as they relate to bullet journaling. A quick search will produce several free results.

Once visual note-takers practice more frequently, watch their confidence grow and notice how much lettering shows up on their notebooks and papers. Encourage students to notice lettering and environmental print on signs, product packaging, publications, posters, t-shirts, and more. Lettering exists all around us making it a great conversation to have with students because everyone can access some form of it in their lives. What styles catch their eye? Colors? Combinations?

Have students practice writing words and sentences quickly, then slow down and rewrite the text using their nicest handwriting. Reflect on the differences between the two, and the importance of being able to write legibly, even in these days of evolving technological competencies.

One more tip on handwriting. Use it as an action research opportunity: studies have shown that taking notes by hand is more effective at encoding information and that students who take notes longhand score better on tests. Why not use this as another purpose for taking visual notes and handwriting the words? Do students notice a difference in their interpretation vs when they type notes or just fill in the blanks of PowerPoint notes? Is there a noticeably better level of understanding? Why? What are they doing differently? Pushing students to be metacognitive, to think about their thinking, will encourage them to become more independent learners who know what works best for them and why. Sometimes, that's even more valuable than the content we are trying to impart.

handwriting

START WITH YOUR OWN NATURAL HANDWRITING

A B C D E F G H I J K L M N O P Q R S T U V W X Y Z → UPPER CASE

a b c d e f g h i j k l m n o p q r s t u v w x y z → lower case

a b c d e f g h i j k l m n o p q r s t u v w x y z → cursive

WHAT QUALITIES DO YOU LIKE MOST?

PRACTICE ONE OR TWO FONTS TO WRITE QUICKLY

abcdefghijklmnopqrstuvwxyz
ABCDEFGHIJKLMNOPQRSTUVWXYZ
abcdefghijklmnopqrstuvwxyz

FAST FONTS WILL LOOK VERY DIFFERENT

FONT INSPIRATION:

WORD DOC FONTS

- TYPE OUT THE ENTIRE ALPHABET IN UPPER & LOWERCASE
- MAKE THE FONTS LARGE ENOUGH TO TRACE FOR PRACTICE

- SIGNAGE
- MAGAZINES
- CHALKBOARDS
- TRADER JOE'S
- SHIRT LOGOS, ETC.

café 24 HRS

SIGNS

EXAMPLES ARE EVERYWHERE!

SCHOOL

WENDI PILLARS @Wendi322

—65—

Icons & Symbols

We are in an age of apps and symbols, infographics, and increasingly linguistically diverse societies which means it's a necessary skill for our teams and learners to become fluent in both text and imagery. Visual literacy must include not only "reading" nonlinguistic symbols, but also "writing" and creating them, not only reading between others' visual lines, but also creating equally evocative images of our own.

When we begin imagining how to represent ideas visually, we want to consider what communicates information quickly but in a way that is recognizable. That's where icons and symbols come in and they are an ideal start point. Even though some of them might seem cliché, they are extensively, even globally, familiar which helps others make meaning and connection.

Icons, from the Greek "eikon," are simple images similar to the shape they represent. This makes them nearly instantly recognizable, like a camera icon on your phone, a shopping cart on your favorite webpage, or that snowflake on your weather app. They are easy to read and clearly resemble the physical items.

Symbols on the other hand are images whose meaning must be learned, such as the bald eagle for America or a cross for Christianity. There may not be any really visible resemblance to the object they represent, and they may be very personal or culturally grounded. As you sketch in your classroom some symbols may even be generated while discussing a specific topic, a type of shorthand to represent what you are learning together. Kraken tacos, for example, (yes, really) resulted from some recent classroom interactions, representing new food combinations during a lesson on food trucks, and now that has become a symbol for "taking chances" and "trying something new!"

Visual notes are an ideal vehicle for comparing literal and symbolic meaning, for example in a single assignment, students signified the word "ancient" with a spiderweb, Egyptian pyramid, old person with a cane, and a pirate ship, among others. Each was symbolic and opened up discussion with details and insights we would otherwise have missed.

Remain flexible because you never know what will transpire. Which would be considered icons on the following page? Symbols? What common icons and/or symbols show up consistently in your business lingo? In your teaching? Which can you add? Which might relate to your information today? How can icons and symbols help ensure your business is understood better?

Icons & Symbols

Kraken Tacos, anyone?

"ancient"

"joy"

BUILDS VISUAL LIBRARY

EMPHASIZES POWER of VISUALS and THEIR MYRIAD INTERPRETATIONS

IDEAS:

PROVIDE ICONS & SYMBOLS FOR YOUR STUDENTS:
⇒ WHAT ARE THEY? (LITERALLY)
⇒ WHAT COULD THEY REPRESENT?

BOOK	COMPUTER	SCHEDULE	LIGHT
Learning	Tech	notebook	HOPE
escape	connection	calendar	POSSIBILITY
TORTURE	online BIZ	TEST	SURVIVAL
GOAL	social media	Journal	Quiet

... ETCETERA ....

☆ ALTERNATIVELY, PROVIDE the WORDS and SEE WHAT THEY COME UP WITH VISUALLY.

WENDI PILLARS @ WENDI322

—67—

Introduce Visual Thinking Into Your Meetings

Psst . . . hey. Leading a meeting anytime soon? Here are three ways to introduce visuals into your meetings.

Paint done. Be crystal clear about what "done" looks like. This phrase and concept come from Brene Brown's *Dare to Lead* and is an antidote to clarifying expectations. We've all been there, where we have expectations that are crystal clear in our own mind, yet we've never voiced them to others. Maybe it was a personal situation, maybe professional. Inevitably, frustration ensued and most likely the required expectation(s) were never achieved. When you ask someone to Paint Done, however, you are asking to see a picture of what success looks like in a holistic view. It invites thinking from others who will be involved in the work, giving them the opportunity to make sure they have what they need to do what is being asked of them. Reality check, space to tackle tough conversations, and authentic collaboration? Check.

Provide a central image, whether it is of your customer, ideal client, employee, or even the competition. It does not have to be fancy and in fact, you might be amazed at the power of your stick figures to finesse conversations. Using an image recalibrates your thinking by tapping into the visual brain. The central figure serves as a neutral anchor for everyone's focus, and your group can use it in multiple ways, even virtually.

In practice, you can use breakout rooms for groups to respond to your prompt. Let's say you're reconfiguring your ideal customer during times of COVID-19. Rather than elicit ideas from a huge group, smaller groups can converse, then you can see where the overlapping ideas among teams exist and where disparities reside. Enter greater thought diversity. Alternatively, a second idea is to ask teams to annotate directly onto the screen using the text feature, typing out descriptive phrases. The anonymity of this feature may be a comfortable boost to those who want to speak against the tide, allowing you to gain real feedback you wouldn't otherwise glean from a larger, inhibited "public" group.

Co-create a visual library. Choose ten icons or simple sketches to represent concepts you are continually discussing, challenges you are facing, aspects you are celebrating, and more. The co-creation piece can be done within set organizational teams, OR among different teams that don't typically work together for cross-pollination of ideas. Once you have those common shared images, they can be used as shortcuts in meetings, on organizational material (newsletters, memos, PR materials, etc.), during mentor/ mentee meetings, as building blocks to spur greater creativity, or to enhance communication among different departments. The resultant shared understanding enlivens conversations, clarifies information, specifies requests for action, and illuminates processes, all because the focus is more tangible when seeing our words on paper or screen. In other words, use simple visuals to help you drill down to the essence of your meeting by helping you clarify what you want to say, connect the dots, prioritize topics and ideas, and specify next steps.

Warning: once you use visuals to get clear, focused and action-imminent, you'll never go back. Prepare thyself.

3 WAYS to INTRODUCE VISUAL THINKING into YOUR MEETINGS

By WENDI PILLARS
@WENDI322

1 "PAINT DONE"

expectations are VOICED and CLARIFIED

2 PROVIDE a CENTRAL IMAGE

* COMPARE and CONTRAST HONEST FEEDBACK & IDEAS

3 CO-CREATE a VISUAL LIBRARY

* COMMON, TANGIBLE LANGUAGE to STREAMLINE COMMUNICATION
* CO-CREATION = BUY-IN and MORE NUANCED THINKING

Jokes, Word Play & Figurative Language

According to renowned linguist David Crystal[5], nearly two-thirds of jokes depend on some sort of word play, and we also know that the brain thrives on novelty with a touch of surprise. This might explain the popularity and linguistic universality of the use of idioms, metaphors, puns, and other figurative language. That popularity can at once enrich and stymie understanding for our audiences, especially those from different cultures because they must be learned as a special "whole." Translating an idiom word by word is tedious and at the end of it all, you could be hanging by a thread. Worse, you could go down in flames, even after going the extra mile.

They are certainly cryptic pre-packaged bits of information that provide strong mental imagery. We're in luck, though, since the brain loves chunking, and idioms like those above answer that need for chunking quite nicely. Words, puns, idioms, and metaphors are all lexemes, self-contained units for conveying meaning. Researchers have found differences in processing time between literal and idiomatic phrases and have found that both of the brain's hemispheres are activated when interpreting figurative language, including evaluation, comprehension, and emotion. Relying heavily on this type of language may exclude many of your audience members.

Metaphors are like the linguistic sibling of symbols. They represent ideas and provoke strong mental imagery that aids comprehension and understanding with specific words. Our reliance upon symbolic thinking and the use of metaphors in daily life is habitual and something no longer in our conscious approach to the world. If you work with multicultural learners, however, the rampant use of figurative language can be a major comprehension obstacle.

Archetypal symbols carry similar meanings in a universal sense, such as "Mother" Earth, light, darkness, up/down, an axis of a wheel, and a circle, for example. They appear in multiple cultures, many remote and distant enough from each other to preclude thoughts that cultures could have collaborated on the design or meaning. This demonstrates the natural inclination for humans to associate items with other known items and to share that meaning.

Visual puns involve word play and imagery, while visual metaphors use images instead of words to represent a comparison. They are thought to be understood by the right hemisphere long before the more literal-minded left hemisphere can spell out the reasons. It all goes back to that wickedly fast processing of images in our brain, far faster than processing text! Art seems to dissolve the barriers between the hemispheres, weaving the left hemisphere's language-based logic with the more holistic, intuitive thinking associated with the right hemisphere.

Synesthetic metaphors also shed light on how our senses are hardwired to integrate their information. Synesthesia is a fascinating mingling of our senses. Some people might taste lemon when they touch metal or earwax when they hear someone's name. Others might associate temperatures, numbers, letters, or words with textures or sounds. Before thinking that's strange, you might be a synesthete, too. (Ever consider a color to be "warm" or "cool?") After all, cross-modal connections are the name of the game.

Drawing out word play and figurative language visually is a powerful way to make learning stick, explore different cultures and norms, and provide opportunities to clarify understanding.

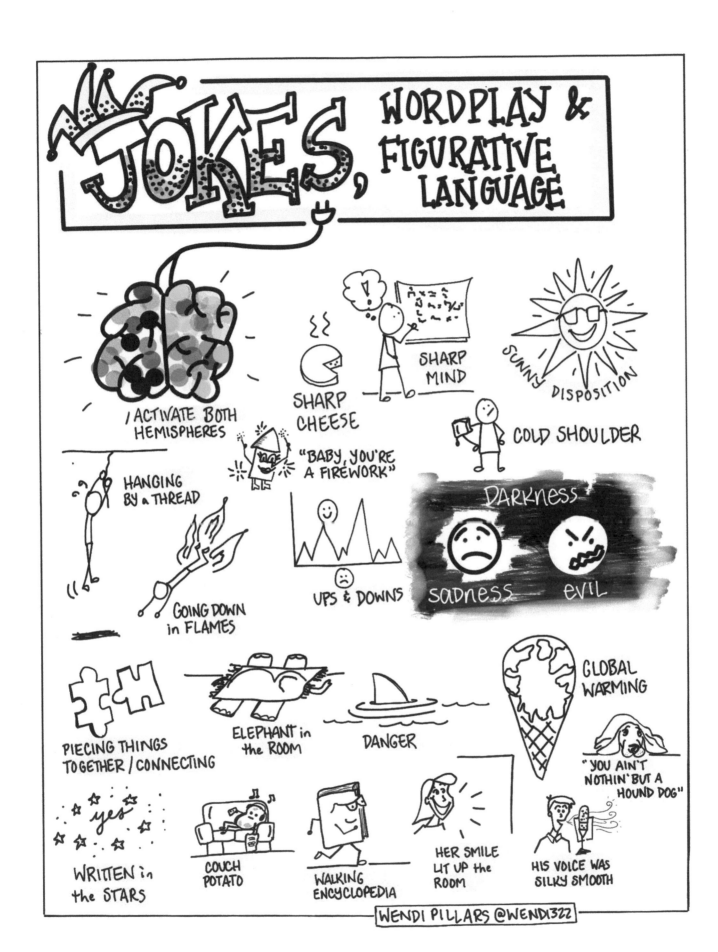

JOKES, WORDPLAY & FIGURATIVE LANGUAGE

ACTIVATE BOTH HEMISPHERES

SHARP CHEESE

SHARP MIND

SUNNY DISPOSITION

COLD SHOULDER

HANGING BY a THREAD

"BABY, YOU'RE A FIREWORK"

GOING DOWN in FLAMES

UPS & DOWNS

DARKNESS
sadness   evil

PIECING THINGS TOGETHER / CONNECTING

ELEPHANT in the ROOM

DANGER

GLOBAL WARMING

"YOU AIN'T NOTHIN' BUT A HOUND DOG"

WRITTEN in the STARS
yes

COUCH POTATO

WALKING ENCYCLOPEDIA

HER SMILE LIT UP the ROOM

HIS VOICE WAS SILKY SMOOTH

WENDI PILLARS @WENDI322

—71—

Just Get Started

This is a basic overview for those who are thinking about getting started with visual notes but are hesitant. It is a great one-pager that answers a lot of questions colleagues have had over the years about "why" visual notetaking should be used, along with tips for success.

READY to TRY VISUAL NOTES?

JUST GET STARTED...

WENDI PILLARS @WENDI322

TITLE • BORDER/CONTAINER • DIVIDERS • SHADOWS

CONTENT

☆ KEY FOCUS?

☆ PURPOSE of NOTES?
- practice only
- for oneself
- for a team/group (problem-solving)
- broader/public audience
- individual work or collaborative?
- quick sketch or larger synthesis

"SKETCHING WHY?" — KNOW YOUR WHY

HIERARCHY

□ LARGER, BOLDER FONTS for MAIN IDEA(s) — BULLETS

□ Smaller, thinner letters for details; lower case

COLOR

♪ BLACK or DARK BASE COLOR

♪ ONE or TWO STRATEGIC HIGHLIGHT COLORS
- company/school colors?
- content-related colors?

♪ COMPLEMENTARY COLORS — COLOR WHEEL GOODNESS

❀ AESTHETICS & ICONS

- LEGIBLE WRITING
- WHITE SPACE
- BORDERS/BORDER LINES
- SHADOWS
- LAYOUT/FLOW of CONTENT

MINDSET

- GROWTH PROCESS
- COMPARE ONLY w/OWN WORK
- KEEP TRACK of PROGRESS
- PRACTICE & OBSERVE
- ❀ PROCESS over PRETTY

• SKETCH YOUR THOUGHTS... CHANGE YOUR FUTURE •

Kinesthetics

I've learned enough in recent years to understand that famously touted learning visual, auditory, and kinesthetic learning styles are a neuromyth, despite what textbooks have printed for decades. Yes, it's okay for learners to reflect on how they learn best and why, but there's huge risk in squashing someone into a single style for the sake of alleged learning efficiency. Our brain craves information from any input available. Without experiencing different types of input, our brains would not be able to optimize their own abilities, nor would our learners be able to develop fully. If we only taught or presented information to a person's strengths—if that were the case—we would simply be missing the point of education.

Yes, I know that the idea of differentiating our daily practices to meet the myriad needs of our learners and clients may be a celebrated idea, but a learning styles questionnaire isn't the way to do it. I believe that everyone benefits from receiving input in multiple modalities that include visual, auditory, and kinesthetic pathways.

My inclusion of *kinesthetics* in this book drills down to the basic physicality of learning, whether it's someone's strength or not. It can relate to the hand movements of sketching: smaller sketches and writing use only the fingers, slightly larger movements involve the wrist, while great big sketches can involve the entire arm and upper body. Hand-eye coordination comes into play, as do basic levels of bodily coordination and stamina.

Employ the use of chart paper or whiteboards for larger sketches. Using larger arm movements, particularly if they cross the midline, helps invigorate cross-hemispheric interaction in our brains. Add movement. Get participants up and moving in a gallery (walk) sketch where each person adds a detail to a sketch then rotates. Have them draw on large paper on a table, with chairs pushed away so they have to stand and view their work from an entirely different angle than if they were seated. Put paper on the floor in your room or in the hallway. Use clipboards and sit outside for a spell. Ask learners to draw with their non-dominant hand. Play music with an upbeat tempo in the background while they are sketching, if appropriate to the topic at hand. Allow learners to sketch in a small group where they each have to contribute on the paper with their own colors, forcing them to share space, coordinate movements, and take turns.

The simple point is, movement and angles of perspective are especially important, even more now, in my opinion. The more we encourage our audience to move, even if for only a few minutes at a time, the greater the benefit to their learning both physically and mentally.

kinesthetics

TRY neon DRY-ERASE MARKERS on the WINDOWS

LARGE BODY MOVEMENTS JUST BY ADDING a BIGGER canvas

USE CHALK OUTSIDE for a LARGE canvas in FRESH air

REVIEW

PLAY MUSIC THEY can move to

WHAT OBJECTS in nature can THEY USE to REPRESENT THEIR LEARNING?

PUSH CHAIRS AWAY for ALL-HANDS-ON-DECK PARTICIPATION

*STUDENTS can WRITE on TABLES WITH DRY-ERASE MARKERS, TOO

WENDI PILLARS @ WENDI322

Language Development Support

Above all else, I am a language teacher. I'm not, nor have I ever been an art teacher. This is why there is so much in this book that not only promotes the thinking side of visual notes, but also listening, reading, writing, and speaking. All of us are technically language teachers, because we build skills in the specific language of our content for communication. Consider any aspects of language unique to your content topic as they are your start point for developing a visual library of icons and symbols to help others remember, recall, retell, and share critical information.

We just need to consider some things along the way.

How does language development occur in your teaching and learning contexts? How does it impact literacy development and understanding? How many speakers of different languages are in front of you on any given day? Where are misconceptions? Which events can be crafted into a timeline? Which words have multiple meanings? How can you use visuals to help your audience comprehend more information, or even some information better? What cultural lens is being used with the language?

As presenters and formal or informal educators, everyone should aspire to include a few activities that can be enhanced with quick sketches or with sketches that are built upon over time. Here are some interactive basics:

- Encourage all participants to speak at least once. It's not always possible, but having that as a goal should be powerful impetus. When learners explain a quick sketch to a partner, that single minute might be more than they talk all day in classes or meetings.

- Everyone should read something, independently, with a partner, or even in whole group. Eyes should be on some sort of text each day. Summarizing a portion of the reading with a sketch, developing vocabulary stories, or creating a quick portrait of a character/historical figure with details will take a little more time but the information will stick a lot longer.

- Aim for participants to write after each session together, whether it be an exit ticket, a synthesizing phrase with their visual notes, a solid sentence, or something more elaborate. Short bursts of sketches with words and phrases make their thinking tangible and hold them accountable on an individual level.

- Word awareness is one of the easiest activities to incorporate, but one we take for granted. There is a tremendous vocabulary gap among our learners and their knowledge can be sporadic. Take time to determine key words and phrases that someone in a particular position, role or level of expertise would use with the content you are presenting. Which words would help summarize a text or other information? How can you and your learners create an interactive word wall to help them be more successful?

The significance of all of these ideas is that your audience is *producing* language in multiple domains. The more different participants are from us, the more we have to learn about them, and the best way to do so is for them to show us what they know, visuals included.

LANGUAGE DEVELOPMENT SUPPORT:

CONSIDER KEY WORDS & IDEAS

❝ Communicate through your content ❞

❝ Make space for inquiry & conversation ❞

❝ Encourage interaction ❞

❝ Encourage other languages ❞

❝ Encourage use of precise vocabulary ❞

❝ How does a person in your field/role/context communicate effectively? ❞

❝ Consider listening, speaking, reading, and writing and how they can share what they learn ❞

❝ What can they create with their new language? ❞

Listening,
Part 1: Tips for Visual Thinkers

Listening. It's something we all do, day in and day out.

But we suck at it.

Listening is also observing. Listening involves voice, inflections, and even body language. Listening well means listening to the said and the unsaid. Listening for opinion versus fact. Listening to paraphrase or to catch words with precision, to extract big takeaways and smaller ones. Listening for jokes, humor, and tone. Listening for what is personal to the speaker and what is a consummate "party line" they may be obligated to say . . .

Listening is complicated which only serves to highlight why we must provide time in our classrooms and meetings for teams and learners to learn how to filter and focus.

I don't expect high school students to know how to take notes when they come into my class. It's just not something they're equipped with, so I scaffold and begin by teaching them that learning how to listen takes practice. Just as with learning any other skill, start off by chunking it to make it more accessible, be patient, and eventually extend listening stamina.

Be explicit about **why** learners are taking notes, what **purpose** or **specific information** they're listening for and maybe **how** they will need to use those notes later. I often use TED talks, but when it's for listening practice, it's with a progression. The first time, we only listen as they take notes and write down words they hear and any sketches that come to mind. I may play it at seventy-five percent speed at first. Then, they listen again as they watch the TED talk, giving them a second go at revising and adding detail to their notes. Third, we have a group discussion, sharing notes and questions. We will then watch one more time, either individually on their Chromebook or later in the unit, as a type of spiral review and group revisit. How might that look for your context?

Listening practice could be in the form of a virtual or face-to-face guest, it could be recorded or live, or it could be you reading a text out loud. And yes, reading out loud is a best practice for literacy at all ages! The first few times you try specific listening practice—which is probably unusual in a non-language acquisition class, but oh-so-important for your content area—provide support for your visual thinkers with ideas like these:

- Equip learners with key visual vocabulary before listening or provide groups time to create what they predict will be discussed based on a title, picture, or outline.

- Provide the main idea or big ideas and have listeners sketch details for each. Alternatively, you provide details so that students can infer, predict, and analyze information to find those main ideas and sketch them.

- Encourage them to listen for facts and words and to refrain from judgment about what they're hearing, at least for the first listen. Push for curiosity or "I wonder . . ." instead. Later, as your thinkers feel more comfortable, uphold their personality and opinions which may emerge visually. That, my friends, is all part of their style.

Later, as your thinkers feel more comfortable, uphold their personality and opinions which may emerge visually. That, my friends, is all part of their style.

> ## "If you are going to listen, you have to be willing to change."
> — Ecologist Gordon Hempton

Listening:

ACTIVE LISTENING

learning HOW TO listen TAKES practice

LISTENING COMPREHENSION

What words do I hear?
What is important to remember?
What is my purpose for listening?
How can I represent key concepts with a visual?
How can I connect those ideas into a visual story?

TEACHER PROVIDES DETAILS
(or VIRTUAL/ONLINE/F2F GUEST; RECORDED or LIVE)

- PROVIDE MAIN IDEA(s)
- STUDENTS SKETCH DETAILS

- OR, SKETCH DETAILS
- STUDENTS INFER, PREDICT, ANALYZE TO DETERMINE KEY IDEAS

MUST HAVE:
- ★ PURPOSE
- ★ INTENTION & ATTENTION
- ★ RESPONSIBILITY TO REPRESENT SOMEONE'S IDEAS WITH FIDELITY.

MUST BE ABLE TO:
- ★ LISTEN WITHOUT JUDGMENT
- ★ LISTEN IN WONDER
- ★ LISTEN WITH CURIOSITY

EQUIP STUDENTS WITH KEY VOCABULARY/PHRASES BEFORE LISTENING
- ★ PROVIDE TIME TO CREATE SHARED OR INDIVIDUAL VISUAL LIBRARIES

WENDI PILLARS @Wendi322

Listening,
Part 2: Intentional Listening

When we teach our audiences that listening is like a muscle, a part of us that can be strengthened with practice, it can be a game changer. It becomes something we have control over.

Listening is also a choice.

What is most surprising to those who create visual notes while listening in real time is just how hard it can be. There is constant filtering and attention to the speaker's words, emotions, perspectives, and even the audience's reactions to what is said.

Are you listening for metaphors, action verbs, cultural connections, data, facts, or story? Or are you listening for the "in-between" spaces? How does the information help you shape the notes you are taking? Are you writing every detail or key words only? Are you sketching while listening or focusing on the verbal first? Are you able to remain neutral, as a mere conduit for what you are hearing or do your biases come charging through? What are you noticing about yourself as you're listening? Are the notes for you or for others?

Visual notetaking can be a one-and-done experience, or it can be something more dynamic and reflective, morphing with new information and insights into connections. The critical piece to realize here is how intentional listening must become for a note taker to be successful.

In the world of visual notetaking, listening goes above and beyond art and deserves its own explicit practice and teaching.

Keep practicing.

Listening:

We have LISTENING MUSCLES → DEVELOPED with PRACTICE & INTENTIONAL FILTERS

Where do <u>students</u> believe it would be valuable to focus their listening?

CHOOSE a FOCUS

☆ Students' purpose
☆ type of information
  • challenges?   • opinions?
  • big ideas?   • solutions?
  • supporting details?   • facts?

FACTS vs. OPINION

☆ personal interpretation?
☆ humor?   ☆ experience?
☆ perspective?   ☆ personality?

REFLECT

☆ listening lens or filter
☆ choice or assignment
☆ influence on their notes?

CONNECTIONS and PATTERNS

☆ Similarities and differences
☆ Dialogue, context, type of content, universal storyline

LISTENING is a CHOICE

WENDI PILLARS @Wendi322

Listening,
Part 3: Interpretations & Ideas

One of the most fascinating attributes of listening is just how proof-positive it is that even though everyone in the room receives the same exact input (i.e., a lecture, story, keynote), sketch interpretations are always so different. The output may have the same or similar information, but rarely is it organized or represented the same.

Like I said, fascinating. A fun and easy activity to illustrate (pun intended) our different interpretations is to dictate sentences for students to draw a simple scene. Students will listen and draw short sentences to practice basic vocabulary, directions, and prepositions (the lamp is to the right of the door, the dog is sitting in front of the refrigerator, the city is in between the forest and the river, above, on top, below, to the east of, north of, behind, next to, etc.), and all with an intermingling of content vocabulary. Students will quickly see how our output differs and how background knowledge comes into play when representing the same topic.

There are plenty of ideas for our business partners, colleagues, and learners to practice the skill of listening beyond listening to the presenter or facilitator, each other, or an in-person guest speaker. Technology ensures there is no shortage of stories, narratives, newscasts, TED talks, podcasts, YouTube how-tos, read-alouds on different literacy sites, and so much more. Choose what is appropriate for your audience, then have them listen to just part of it or all of it at once. Pause the speaking at pre-selected points and make predictions. Play the beginning and the end portions and ask them to create a middle. Be creative.

Sketch the speaker sight unseen. What details matter? What assumptions and biases surface? What value do we place on visual cues? This can be a sensitive topic for some, so be mindful and prepared for conversations around bias, stereotypes, and the power of assumptions. Compare ideas with peers and then show an actual photo of the speaker. If possible, reach out to the speaker to share what you learned, not only from the talk, but about the results of the sketching exercise. What surprised them? What made it easy to do? Difficult?

Listen more than once. Listen at different speeds. Listen for specific purposes, something different or more specific each time. Share interpretations and work with each other. What rationale and reasoning do students have to support their visual representations? Even the simplest imagery can evoke powerful responses, so remember never to judge someone's "art." Ask students to tell you more or what prompted them to hone in on a certain detail. Even a few minutes of practice a day will help enforce this essential skill.

Practice.

Listening:

LISTEN to PART of a STORY, NARRATIVE, TED Talk, NEWSCAST, PODCAST,...

⏸ *pause it*

THEN SKETCH PREDICTIONS.

What happens next?
WHO, WHAT, WHERE, HOW?, etc.

BUILD UPON EACH OTHERS' IDEAS

- Listen to others' descriptions
- ADD & REVISE information using EVIDENCE, RATIONALE, REASONING
- How are others' interpretations DIFFERENT or SIMILAR to yours?

WHY?

SKETCH the SPEAKER SIGHT UNSEEN

VALUE of VISUAL CUES
ASSUMPTIONS

ACCENTS
DETAILS that MATTER

- Conversation starter for bias, stereotypes, power of assumptions
- What prompted you to draw x, y, z details?
- Compare with peers THEN with actual photo of speaker
- ⬆ SHARE images and thinking with actual speaker

MAKE NEW CONNECTIONS IN LIGHT of REASONING & EVIDENCE.

- listen to speakers <u>and</u> peers' interpretations
- listen AGAIN for SPECIFIC PURPOSES:
  - more detail
  - specific evidence
  - interesting facts
  - new details
  - word usage,

  etc....

fascinating PROOF-POSITIVE that the SAME INPUT ≠ SAME OUTPUT

WENDI PILLARS @Wendi322

Mapping

There is growing recognition that spatial literacy (mapping and spatial thinking) is now as important as mathematical literacy (numeracy) and classic literacy (ability to read and write).[6]

As a visual, maps have an abundance of entry points for viewers to explore ideas, situations, current events, and more within the world around us. Spatial perspectives can serve as a framework to interpret and question what we're listening to, reading, and watching. We want to make certain our learners gain confidence with map skills and spatial thinking beyond the GPS and Google Maps on their phones.

Learning to ask where something is and why it is there essentially shifts thinking from the page to the world. In its basic sense a map is a representation or a picture of a place, shown with symbols, within a certain context. Through maps we can see relationships, sizes, locations, distances, and land features. They can be extremely detailed or show larger patterns and distributions, any of which can be used to develop students' spatial thinking related to global and local spaces and places. If there's a preposition in your content, chances are there's a map just waiting to be discovered.

When someone actually draws maps, it helps them envision a setting more clearly, understand how an issue might unfold, or analyze a problem through a unique lens. This is more about drawing a picture, this is analysis in the moment as participants work through charts, numbers, estimations, timelines, and overlays to decipher problems and solutions using spatial thinking. Reading about migration is good. Recreating a map with topographical features throughout a migrant's journey is better. Learning about terraced farming in Nepal is good. Understanding the type of landscape that demands this ingenuity is better.

During spatial thinking our brain relies upon its powers of comparison: how does this relate to what I already know? Spatial thinking helps us categorize places based on what nearby regions have in common in order to make the information more memorable, and it helps us both seek and create patterns through closer observation. How can you use these patterns and categories to enhance learning? What creates a "sense of place?" Dive into those historical places, those fictional settings, those inspirational homesteads of authors, scientists, athletes . . . Read, use, and analyze maps, then recreate them and take artistic license with your interpretative gifts.

What's your vision for future learning? What format will best link the disparate pieces and make it comprehensible? Will spatial thinking become a part of your repertoire? What kind of mapping can your students and teams create to frame a richer understanding of different people and places in our world, both what they know and what they learn?

INCLUDE a MAP

DIVE INTO a "SENSE of PLACE"

★ CHOOSE a LOCATION
- hometown of a character, scientist, mathematician?
- place of inspiration for author, scientist, historian?
- place YOU know and love

...ETC.,....

★ CHOOSE KEY SITES
- context-based
- sites? experiences? activities?
- source(s) of inspiration

★ ACTUALLY LOCATE SITES
- use Google maps or an ArcGIS platform to get an overview of your locations, distances, landscapes, and more

★ SKETCH ICONS
- represent each location, activity or experience with an icon

★ REMEMBER YOUR TITLE
- where does it fit?
- where does it make sense to go?
- are there multiple place names to consider? (political, historical, etc.)

FEEL FREE TO:
- include words and phrases with each icon
- color code icons, outlines, lettering
- distort the map to meet your needs
- zoom in or zoom out as needed
- take ARTISTIC LICENSE because this is YOUR interpretation

★ INCLUDE MAP "EYE CANDY"
- legend, key
- color-code
- theme
- compass rose
- border
- inset map, ETC.,...

WENDI PILLARS @Wendi322

Metacognition

Make sure visual notetaking is not just another activity you assign. Metacognition is, in its simplest definition, "thinking about thinking" or the process of evaluating our own thinking. There's no better time to instill metacognitive awareness than when learners have the opportunity to decelerate.

Providing crucial time to process what your audience is learning is the special sauce behind this type of notetaking but it's also a time to let learners know visual notes are only ONE strategy, ONE tool they have in their respective learning toolkits. It may not be for everyone all the time for every content every day. No strategy is, as far as I'm aware. This one is no different.

But maybe, just maybe, visual notetaking can be useful for them some of the time. Our role as responsible leaders and educators is to show how to learn with varying approaches for taking notes and how to keep track of what they are learning. It is ultimately the learners' responsibility to determine if, when, and how a particular strategy works for them.

Encourage visual thinkers to revisit their visual notes and reflect whether they are more likely to return to these notes than linear, words-only notes. Are the notes useful for expanding ideas with new information? Set up times for them to retell what they've learned, one or two weeks later to see how much they remember. Do they feel it's easier to explain something once they've sketched it out? Why do they think that is? Do they believe their skills have evolved? How does that make them feel? Can someone else explain their notes?

What was easy and what was difficult for you as you listened or read and sketched? What can you do differently the next time? What made it successful for you and how can you continue this good work? How will this help you in other contexts, with other peers or clients?

As they compare and contrast their notes with peers, highlight how identical input does not equal identical output or takeaways. Again, why do they think that is? Is it anyone's fault? What insights do they hold about focus and attention? What characterizes your thought sifting process—can you identify any patterns in your notes over time?

What we call higher-order thinking, neuroscientists call executive function. Metacognitive awareness takes us all one step closer to becoming self-directed learners with more developed executive functioning. With guidance and practice, those who examine their learning experiences can more readily link the causes and effects of participation, studying, and activating memory from separate storage regions in the brain.

Why wouldn't we teach our learners more about how to learn so they can get better at the "what" to learn?

Modifications

In case you know anyone who really struggles with visual notetaking or visual thinking, this page is for you.

First, I want to reiterate that this notetaking style is a skill, which means it can be developed over time. With practice, we can all improve and there will always be room for improvement!

Secondly, check motivation through your objectives. Is there a clear purpose for your audience as they take their notes? Are they listening/reading for main ideas? Vocabulary? Information to compare and contrast, summarize, predict, or synthesize? How much detail is expected?

Third, who will the audience be for the visual notes? This definitely impacts motivation!

We all need to encourage our learners and audiences to have and build strategies and self-advocacy skills when they are unable to, or simply don't understand everything they hear or read. Here are some tips that I've found useful with my learners of all ages:

- Have learners work with a partner or small group after the listening task so they can compare notes and clarify information.

- Have successful note-takers and sketchers share their strategies for taking notes, finding and capturing the essence.

- Get learners used to listening and reading for the gist—or a particular piece of information—and have them represent it via sketching, rather than multiple pieces.

- Use repeated listening or reading to focus on adding details.

- Encourage multiple formats, such as reading a text to a partner before reading it independently or listening to a video before watching it.

- Frontload vocabulary or key terms with a collective visual bank of sketches. Elicit possible representations from the class for even the most abstract words to get their minds in gear. Not having to think up ideas for a few words will build confidence and alleviate anxiety with this strong start point.

- Be open and aware of when someone's knowledge is activated and they feel empowered to take a different direction with their notes.

- Insert an element of competitive rivalry—volunteers can take their place at the whiteboard or with paper at their seats. Read a selection or part of a selection (or have another student read!) while the volunteers sketch simultaneously. Analyze who captured the most key points and practice providing constructive feedback.

- Provide time to share, modify, or confirm what they have on their papers.

- Provide sentence frames to use as they retell what is on their sketches, perhaps a "why" behind their choices, and maybe even a "how" they organized their work.

- Conduct a group after-action review to determine what worked. What suggestions do they have to make it better the next time? What information was routinely missed? Emphasized? Captured? It's all such delicious feedback for leaders and educators to understand learners' thinking!

Negative Space

Also known as "white space," negative space is the space around objects and text that permeates your visual. Counterintuitively, the "nothingness" can still act as a guide showing your eyes where to look and where to–there's no better way to say it–breathe. Looking at the two examples on the following page, you can see the differences. One has a lighter feel than the other.

Characteristics that help with the lightness of the top image are thinner lines, a simple palette, and most of all, negative space. This is a collection of facts, rather than a flowchart so there's not a specific direction to move. Neither is there a need for hierarchy so there are no lists, no numbered bullets, no other bold headings beside the title, so the eye is free to float and explore at will. Borders are used minimally, but each fact is accompanied by one image for a 1:1 ratio. It was created asynchronously, meaning that I had time to sit with facts and create a list of ideas first from quite a bit of research information. Sometimes that is helpful–to have the time, that is–but it's also more difficult because there aren't any excuses for leaving something out or not portraying something accurately.

The second image was created synchronously, as I listened to Dr. Tyrone Howard speak. If you are familiar with him, he is a fast-talker with very little fluff. He is a hard-hitting speaker, and I felt like so much needed to be captured. There are borders around many of the facts to help set them apart, some bulleted lists and obvious groupings of information, along with some color to help ideas stand out. It is far more dense with text, heavy lines, and imagery, but many in the audience were still grateful to have this reminder as a content refresh simply because his keynote was so jam-packed with thought-provoking ideas. They'd already forgotten much of his wisdom by the end of the speech because he'd said so much!

How many classes or meetings do we have that are the same? The ones where our audience and learners are lucky to walk away with one or two concepts . . . After. All. That. Work. And planning.

As it was a synchronous capture on a single piece of foam core board, I'm okay with how it turned out. It's not perfect, but it's useful and even after time, reading this transports me right back to that packed conference room as Dr. Howard fired up the crowd.

When perfection is pitted against making things memorable and accessible to others, the latter reigns in my book any day. Feel free to read that again, to yourself, and your learners. Purpose and process will always drive your outcome.

negative space

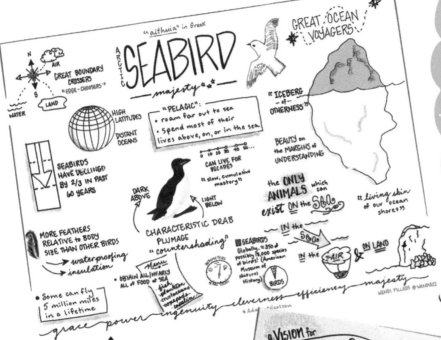

negative space or "WHITE SPACE" HELPS the BRAIN & the eyes BREATHE

← CREATED asynchronously for PERSONAL LEARNING

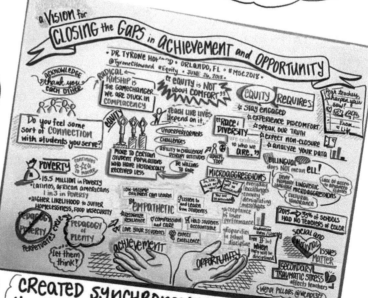

CREATED SYNCHRONOUSLY, WHILE the Speaker was Talking.

"LIGHTER"
- MORE WHITE SPACE
- THINNER LINES
- MINIMAL COLOR USE

"HEAVIER"
- VERY DENSE INFORMATION
- DARKER LINES
- NOT SURE WHERE TO LOOK or HOW INFORMATION FLOWS
- VERY LITTLE NEGATIVE SPACE!

WENDI PILLARS @WENDI322

Neuroscience,
Part 1: Brain Magic

Despite theories of people being right-brained or left-brained, it's important to realize that there is continual interplay between the brain's two hemispheres. Both hemispheres support our thinking while visual notetaking marries the hemispheres nicely, born of auditory, visual, and kinesthetic strengths, while zipping information back and forth between the lobes in a process of synthesis. Any attempt to view the brain in motion as separate entities greatly oversimplifies its endless activities and abilities.

Some research shows that seventy-five percent of our incoming information is processed visually. That's some pretty savvy cognitive processing and as someone seeking ways of reaching our audience, we'd be CRAZY not to acknowledge it. Other research claims a lower percentage, but it's still *much* greater than the other senses: "the machinery that accomplishes these tasks is by far the most powerful and complex of the sensory systems. The retina . . . is actually an outgrowth of the brain[7] . . . [and] neurons devoted to visual processing take up about fifty percent of the cortex" (as opposed to a mere eight percent for touch and three percent for hearing).

Science has shown that our brain is what sees rather than the eyes. In essence, when we think, we see and we imagine. We imagine things we've never even seen all the time or we picture all kinds of things that are not in our vision pathway. If we hear or read a word, an image comes to mind; we are immersed in imagery and it's so automatic that we don't pay attention to what is happening in our thinking.

Yet we need to. Visual notetaking helps us do that, to build upon our visual thinking.

Visuals that we create tap into a confluence of all that lies in our personal background and educational experience. Emotions may be integrated and other sensory cues such as the weather, sounds, and smells associated with an image. Context, people, judgments (or not) all come into play, it is instantaneous, and it is nowhere near exactly like another person's image even if you were considering the same word, phrase, or other input.

As a presenter or educator, you know there's a boatload of content to get through, but it's well worth your time to use images when you are teaching. Our brains are masters at remembering pictures: studies show that when you hear a piece of information, you'll recall about ten percent of it three days later.[8] If you add a picture to that information for your audience, they'll be able to recall nearly sixty-five percent.

Ten percent versus sixty-five percent? A fifty-five percent chance of increased recall *just by adding a picture?* I don't know about you, but hot-diggety, I'd say that's definitely worth my time as a presenter or educator! It makes my job a whole lot easier and a lot more interesting. This includes artwork, photographs, other primary sources, and generating visuals by sketching. Simply put, greater learning and understanding occur with visual support.

Brain  Magic

ABOUT **75%** OF OUR BRAIN'S SENSORY PROCESSING CAPACITY IS DEDICATED to **VISION**

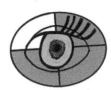

LEARNERS **REMEMBER** up to **55% MORE** IF WE INCLUDE A VISUAL

VISUALS TAP INTO MULTIPLE RETRIEVAL PATHS; REMEMBERING AN IMAGE ACTUALLY RECONSTRUCTS KNOWLEDGE FROM ALL of THOSE DIFFERENT PATHWAYS.

IMAGES ARE PROCESSED 60,000 TIMES **FASTER** THAN TEXT.

MUCH OF OUR NEW INFORMATION DISAPPEARS WITHIN THE FIRST HOUR AFTER LEARNING IT, UNLESS IT'S APPLIED, MANIPULATED, OR ACCOMPANIED BY A VISUAL.

WENDI PILLARS @Wendi322

Neuroscience,
Part 2: Tips for Better Recall

Here's some cool information. Learners tend to be best at recalling the first and last chunks of new information we share with them. Neuroscientists refer to this as the *primacy-recency* effect. For those of us accustomed to using the beginning of a meeting, speech, or class for thank yous, a review, or house-keeping, it seems counterintuitive to think that new information presented first has the best chance of being recalled (due to primacy), while the last information presented has the next best chance of recall (due to recency). Those who study learning cycles also suggest that some sort of consolidation needs to occur about every twenty minutes or so.

Other than using two to three-minute sketches for consolidation, what else can leaders and educators do to optimize this understanding of how we learn?

Save the review, thank yous, homework discussion, announcements, and attendance for later in the class period or presentation. Try to ensure the first ten minutes are extremely pointed and explicitly linked to the new lesson. Maybe a couple of those minutes can be predicting with sketches, representing a new concept via sketching, or as a warm-up with the new content. Have students define and visualize (with a sketch) a new word or two that they will encounter that day. This draws in background knowledge and helps them relate what they know while priming their thinking for what lies ahead. Sharing out helps broaden those ideas, but you can still guide the discussion through your choice of the vocabulary used. If you're trying to keep that first ten minutes dedicated to pure listening or absorption of information, postpone a sketch turn until fifteen to twenty minutes in. Keeping a time limit per sketch will help keep pace and focus.

The last five or ten minutes of your presentation or lesson constitute the recency period, ripe for another dose of important information. Use that time for closure, asking participants for a visual synthesis of notable new knowledge, their prediction(s), or some form of a "what if" question. If they've already started a sketch, have them add two or three new details to drive home connections supported by detailed evidence. Perfect for an exit ticket.

I'm not saying you should do all of this in a presentation or class period every single day. If you're like me, maybe you struggle sometimes wrapping up with an exit ticket, let alone getting such timing down. This might seem overwhelming. Instead what I'm suggesting is that using this as a strategy once in a while in one of these ways can really improve your audience's recall and comprehension and your vision of their understanding. On the other hand, if your objective is to have them practice the skill of visualizing, then it could be one heck of a fun day with visuals galore. Embrace the change of pace while taking the time to be metacognitive about it, too. Use these activities to explain why you're doing what you're doing and how our brains prefer to learn. Who knows, they might just see how this helps their understanding and remind you that they need to get busy those first ten minutes or complete an exit ticket to help them remember!

TIPS for BETTER RECALL

PRIMACY-RECENCY EFFECT

☆ NEW INFORMATION PRESENTED FIRST HAS THE BEST CHANCE OF BEING RECALLED (PRIMACY)

☆ LAST INFORMATION PRESENTED HAS THE NEXT BEST CHANCE OF BEING RECALLED (RECENCY)

HOW CAN I USE MY INSTRUCTIONAL START & END TIMES MORE EFFECTIVELY?

CONSOLIDATION

☆ SOME SORT OF CONSOLIDATION NEEDS TO OCCUR ABOUT EVERY 20 MINUTES OR SO.

- 2-3 MINUTE SKETCHES TO REPRESENT WHAT WAS JUST LEARNED
  OR
- NEW VOCABULARY WORD(S) IN CONTEXT
  OR
- PREDICTIONS ABOUT FUTURE INFORMATION/ CONNECTIONS

BUILD UPON KNOWLEDGE

☆ AS STUDENTS LEARN MORE ABOUT A GIVEN TOPIC, HAVE THEM ADD TO THEIR NOTES A LITTLE MORE EACH DAY.

- INDIVIDUALLY
- PARTNERS or SMALL GROUPS
- WHOLE CLASS to CLARIFY INFORMATION OR DEEPEN UNDERSTANDING

ADDITIONAL SKETCHES & DETAILS

HIGHLIGHT OR COLOR-CODE IDEAS

CONNECT IDEAS USING ARROWS OR OTHER CONNECTORS

REVISE INITIAL SKETCHES BASED ON NEW INFORMATION

WENDI PILLARS @Wendi322

Neuroscience,
Part 3: Real Life Applications

"Use it or lose it" is more than a pat phrase in education. Research has shown that if we don't interact with or repeat information somehow after hearing it or reading it, it's likely to be lost within 15-30 seconds. Short-term memory helps you get from the beginning of a sentence or paragraph to the end, but wow, 15-30 seconds if there's no further interaction with material?

From a biological standpoint, all learning is about change, particularly at the neuronal level where learning takes place. At its most effective, learning is an active process, even moreso with visuals. Rather than listen passively to a speaker or lecture, with a single pathway for information to travel into the brain, drawing forces complex decision-making: what to write down, what to draw to represent something, where to draw it on the page, how to connect, group or categorize information, and otherwise reconstruct what they are hearing. This is far different than well-intentioned guided notes in which the audience scans a PowerPoint slide for a highlighted word to fill in the blanks on their own paper.

Multiple pathways are involved when creating visual notes, including the visual, kinesthetic, and semantic (meaning) memories that come with a given idea or word. The more pathways information travels into our brains, the more access points available to recall it later. Drawing helps us focus and manipulate ideas in our minds, processing it numerous ways with greater opportunities to be stored long enough to apply it.

Learning is also influenced by our prior experiences, which is referred to as transfer. When something new is learned and connected to background knowledge, the likelihood of our students remembering more is significantly higher. So, in a meeting or in a class, sit with a topic just a little bit longer, allowing time to consolidate information housed in the brain. Jumping from one topic to another can disrupt a flow of information. Cycle between the abstract and concrete with discussions, visuals, revisions, and reflections to deepen meaning. Giving visual thinkers "permission" to tap into their past learning is also a metacognitive tool; being explicit about the what, why and how of connecting the prior understanding and experiences to new learning values what each person brings to the learning scenarios.

While acknowledging students' prior learning, we also need to make sure we continue to challenge them to grow beyond what they know. *"Ok, great, you know x,y, and z. Now, let's figure out how that plays a role with today's new content and take that knowledge to a new level. Are you with me?"* Hopefully, this helps lower their affective filter at least a little by providing an opportunity for emotions to surface, especially since they play such an immense role when information needs to move into longer-term memory. When "new learning has minimal or no emotional component, the chances of long-term memory consolidation and storage are low."

You can see that making memories is complex, but creating visuals gives all learners one more option to transform input into output that can be used to address an array of needs.

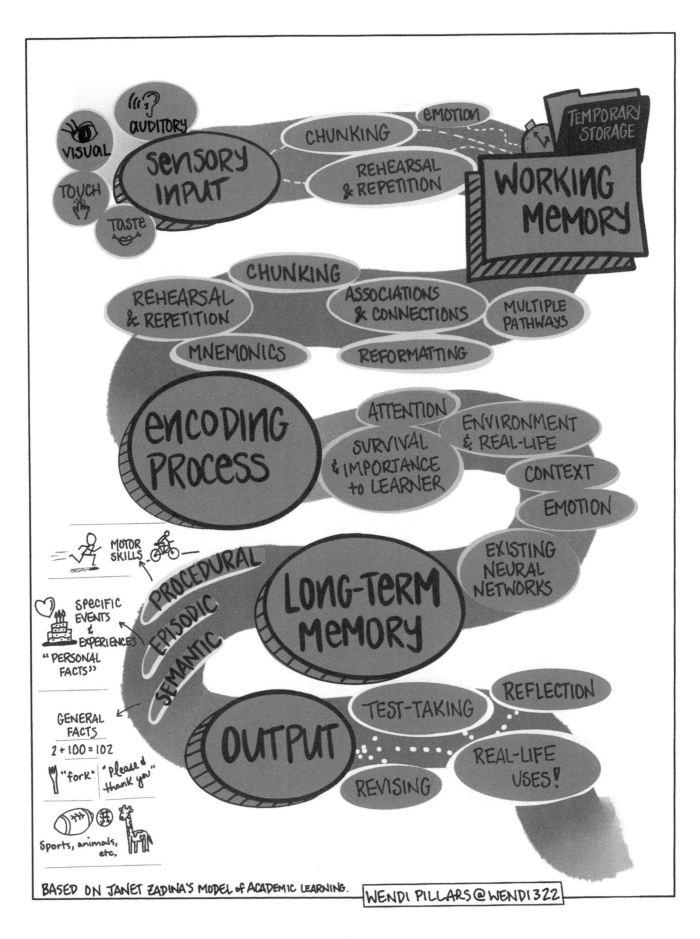

BASED ON JANET ZADINA'S MODEL OF ACADEMIC LEARNING.

WENDI PILLARS @WENDI322

Neuroscience,
Part 4: Making Memories

From the previous pages, we know that our neurons are busy. They're always working, establishing relationships and relevance, determining which memories get through to long-term storage, and which need to do a hasty retreat.

What I love thinking about is how much work our brain does in the work of creating memories and allowing us to retrieve them—with our support. To think that every memory is a reconstruction shaped by new knowledge is mind-boggling. That means if I recall a memory today of my son singing a song in the backyard when he was two, it will be re-encoded with today's context, emotion, and knowledge, twelve years later as he rocks out to a very different type of music. Our memories continually evolve.

Eventually it seems then, that our memories will only contain a glimmer of the originals encoded. Every layer, each pathway we use to remember and recall, will help strengthen them, and the more frequently the better. Here we see the recurring need for connection between the old and the new to make it stick since each new bit of input will need to forge new relationships among our many multitasking neurons.

Teaching others about why we spiral or chunk information, why we present it in multiple formats and look at it from different angles, or why it's important to review previous notes along with notes from the current unit, help cement the idea that we do have some control over our learning abilities. Our learners can be more successful if they understand how their brain learns; being transparent and intentional with our choice of strategies will help lead them to become increasingly independent learners.

"The ENEMY of MEMORY isn't TIME; it's OTHER MEMORIES"

-DAVID EAGLEMAN

WE ALL HAVE a FINITE NUMBER of NEURONS and they all *multitask*

EACH NEW EXPERIENCE or BIT of INPUT NEEDS to ESTABLISH *new relationships* AMONG the FINITE NEURONS

EVERY MEMORY is a *reconstruction* THAT is SHAPED BY NEW KNOWLEDGE YOU HAVE

STRONGER MEMORIES are CREATED WHEN MULTIPLE PATHWAYS are ACCESSED

NEURONS THAT ARE ACTIVE at the SAME TIME = *stronger connections* & MORE PATHWAYS to RETRIEVE THOSE MEMORIES in the FUTURE

LAYER by LAYER OUR MEMORIES SHIFT, CHANGE, STRENGTHEN, and FADE

EACH TIME WE RETRIEVE a MEMORY WE ADD to it OR REVISE it ACCORDING to OUR PRESENT CONTEXT.

OUR NEURONS ARE ALWAYS WORKING!

PHEW!

WENDI PILLARS @Wendi322

Neuroscience,
Part 5: Graphics Create Meaning

Tom Wujec, in his TED Talk "Three Ways the Brain Makes Meaning," touts the powers of graphics and visuals to create powerful learning experiences.

We know that people in general tend to learn better visually (Yapton, 1998), and probably more so now with the onslaught of apps and icons that enter our worlds daily. You've also learned throughout this book that visual notes frequently rely on visual metaphors which boost understanding and how we remember concepts. The visual metaphors and even the colors used in visual notes can tap into our emotional side, too, as we discover what resonates with us the most and how we feel about the way a concept is represented visually. Even mulling over which pieces of information to include in a sketch and how to connect them push us to think about our knowledge more deeply and more intentionally than if we were trying to memorize a bulleted list of facts.

In other words, drawings engage our brains and attention more fully. Ever heard of the Picture Superiority Effect? It basically states that pictures are remembered for longer time periods than words alone; hence, pictures are superior to mere text or the corresponding words. Age can play a factor in recognition memory (how familiar images are can enhance memory), with the picture superiority effect more effective with learners older than seven thanks to life experiences.

Language learners often benefit from seeing pictures alongside text and analyzing images of a topic prior to reading a text because they have time to create supportive mental models. They also benefit from sketching out new vocabulary or phrases and sketching out connections among pieces of information during reading.

Marketers play on our penchant for quick visual information all the time. How quickly do consumers and clients need to see your ads? Do they have time to read a lot of text or would an impactful visual have more mental staying power? How does that translate to internal memos? Outgoing newsletters? Vision and mission planning? Someone taking visual notes of your goals will be a foundational reference for your team members because that visual will be a grounding element from which to build and ideate together.

Regardless of how you incorporate more drawing, visuals will make your conversations more memorable, your content clearer, and if you are drawing in real time, your audience is more likely to understand what is being shared. You are helping others make connections among concepts and ideas, and you are likely going to engage your team in new ways as you make the invisible visible, crafting shared mental models.

To paraphrase Tom Wujec, use images to clarify ideas, interact with images to encourage engagement, and augment your memory/recall with evolving views and understanding. Aren't these goals we all have when learning, presenting, and teaching others?

3 WAYS the BRAIN CREATES MEANING

— Tom Wujec —

HOW DO GRAPHICS CREATE MEANING for our BRAIN?

DORSAL STREAM
- locates objects
- actively navigates
- interactive imagery

PRIMARY VISUAL CORTEX
- simple geometry
- "relay station"

WE MAKE MEANING by seeing
1. use images to CLARIFY ideas
2. interact w/images = ENGAGEMENT
3. augment memory w/ EVOLVING VIEWS

LIMBIC SYSTEM
- deep within brain
- very old
- feels: "gut center"
- pattern-detection

VENTRAL STREAM
- objects
- word association
- engaging & looking at visuals create meaning
- selective logic

"WHAT detector"

"VISUAL PERSISTENCE"

"UNIFIED MENTAL MODEL"

"SHARED SENSE of all PARTS of a PLAN"

"SHARED MENTAL MODELS"

"MAKE INVISIBLE VISIBLE"

WENDI PILLARS @ WENDI3ZZ

—101—

Objectives

I don't have much to add to this visual note, since I wrote about objectives at the beginning of this book. However, this visual outlines example objectives I have for visual thinkers, leaders, educators, and students in a global sense!

What I would like you to analyze is how similar information can be shared in different ways. This one, for example, is similar to what I would share with audiences or students before a presentation or a unit rather than a bullet-point list of words that no one pays attention to. If I had written these phrases out in a list, they would have all run together. Having distinct images already makes it pop, and now when I try to recall the information, I have visual hooks that my recall abilities just love.

What do you notice that could be useful? What would you change? Is there enough negative space? Is the ratio of images to text okay? What could you add to make this a more interactive or more memorable image? And the big question: how could I make my brain dab a little more legit?

How will you present your next set of objectives for your meeting, presentation, or class?

OBJECTIVES:

IDENTIFY YOUR **PURPOSE** & the **MESSAGE** YOU WANT YOUR STUDENTS to WALK AWAY KNOWING.

SHIFT OUR MINDSET FROM "PRESENTING" INFO to TEACHING IT.

ACQUIRE STRATEGIES to **EDUCATE & EMPOWER** STUDENTS LOCALLY and WORLDWIDE.

⤵ ★ REAL-LIFE SKILLS ★

UNDERSTAND BASIC DEVELOPMENTAL CHARACTERISTICS of **DIVERSE LEARNERS.**

Observing closely:
Learning to See Differently

Learning to see differently means that sometimes visual notes can be sketches of an actual phenomenon or object, and slowing down is the magical appeal of this work. When we can sketch and think like a scientist the emphasis remains on recording and communicating without simple or cliché icons.

This type of slow looking gives emphasis to an object or specimen in front of the learner who is tasked with finding particular and unique characteristics. The first time I tried this, we started small and simple—with a blade of grass. We needed six different shades of green to get close to the way the light played upon that single blade. The lines we noticed, the patterns, the designs . . . such incredible intricacies and nuances are to be found. This is not easy to do; few are used to examining anything so closely. Support your learners and audiences by modeling how to look, how to get down on your hands and knees or sit at eye level with their target object, and how to examine it from different sides, how to break it down into smaller pieces. This may or may not be very new for different people, so again, be patient with any initial reluctance.

Conduct a think aloud about what is important to note and why. Talk through your self-doubts if you feel any creative inadequacies surface so that participants start to learn through your doing, how you push through doubts, not just your "saying." Ask questions like: *What growth do you see with your work? How are you noticing more details today? What helped you represent something just a little more accurately? What part of your sketch are you most proud of?*

Provide purpose for your visual thinkers as they observe closely. Choose one or two prompts such as: As you record and draw include colors, shades, and contrasts, even if black and white. Where are the darker and lighter areas? How can you represent those? Are they caused by temporary sunlight or are they permanent markings? Are there other explanations for its shape, form, or location? What if you stand further away? How does your perception change? What happens when you use this magnifying glass? What surprises do you find? Will extra diagrams help you further detail what you see? Maybe a larger cutaway of a pattern, for instance? What specific vocabulary do you need to label your visual once it's finished? What questions do you have about this object now that you've observed it so closely? And so on.

Once learners have finished, it's time for constructive peer feedback. Encouragement is key, as is growth and the ability to respond to the given prompt(s). However, even though it may be the best work a particular learner has achieved in the realm of thinking and sketching like a scientist, provide prompts for reflection like: *What details could you add to make your sketch even more accurate? How might changing the size/angle of your visual enhance the detail? What were you most curious/surprised about as you created your visual? What story do you want your audience to remember about your visual? Why is this important? Why is this important to YOU?*

One-Pager on Visual Thinking

Ever need to explain the value of your product or service for others? Consider using simple visuals to create a single-page summary that makes your organization, product or service stand out from a bulleted list or otherwise text-heavy promotion. Hand-drawn images are still, despite their "simplicity", a powerful messaging tool that appeals to the human side of business and understanding, while fueling your behind-the-scenes processes with new intention.

Co-creating this type of visual summary is an unparalleled discussion and filtering activity. Ask others in your team or organization what THEY think the value is, and what THEY think are the key points that others need to know in order to choose what you have to offer. It is sobering to realize how many different ideas and perceptions are floating around among team members when you believe everyone is on the same page.

Creating a one-page visual summary *literally and tangibly* ensures everyone's thinking is on the same page. In turn, this thinking becomes shareable, and malleable or customizable for different viewers. Obviously your values won't change, but the way you present them for your different clients or audiences can shift. Change colors to match a client's brand, or substitute a couple of words/phrases with an organization's specific synonyms for even more rapid alignment. Perhaps you can include some visuals the target audiences rely upon to build out thinking from their standpoint.

Don't get too attached to your first idea(s) or implementation as you create this type of visual. Make sure to include feedback loops and open communication lines, and be ready to pivot or completely change if required. It does need to capture value along with the core content, aka, the "short story" of your organization/service.

How can your summary connect your high-level concepts to your client's/audience's day-to-day decision-making? How can your summary serve as a tool to help influence organization, communication, and the implementation of new thinking? How can you leverage the potent combination of a creative and structured approach to sharing your business/organizational value with the world?

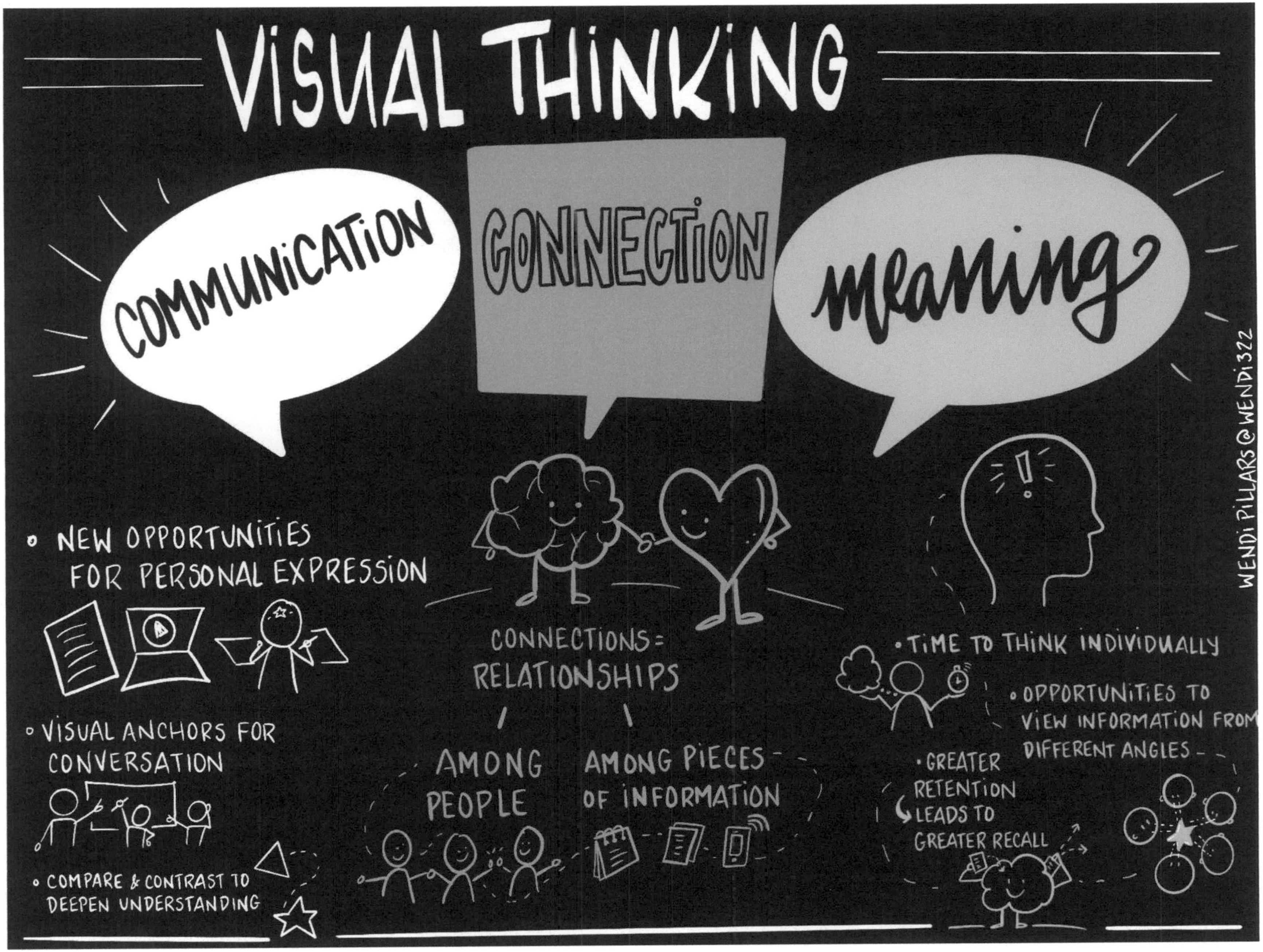
VISUAL THINKING
COMMUNICATION
CONNECTION
MEANING
WENDI PILLARS @WENDI322
• NEW OPPORTUNITIES FOR PERSONAL EXPRESSION
• VISUAL ANCHORS FOR CONVERSATION
• COMPARE & CONTRAST TO DEEPEN UNDERSTANDING
CONNECTIONS = RELATIONSHIPS
AMONG PEOPLE
AMONG PIECES OF INFORMATION
• TIME TO THINK INDIVIDUALLY
• OPPORTUNITIES TO VIEW INFORMATION FROM DIFFERENT ANGLES
• GREATER RETENTION LEADS TO GREATER RECALL

Organization,
Part 1: Hierarchy

How do you know where to start drawing or recording on a page? Start with a title, and then think about your content.

The bigger or more important the idea, the larger the writing or the image on the page. Maybe it's the main idea, maybe it's an idea that evoked the most emotion or got the deepest belly laughs from the audience or the students. Maybe it's simply a name or the title that ends up being the largest element on the page, surrounded by details. Whatever it is, make it stand out somehow in the name of hierarchy.

Change the size of your handwriting to a much larger one, use bold lettering and upper-case lettering instead of lower case to make differences more visual. Exaggerate sizes. Use contrasting color. Draw larger images to capture attention, smaller ones to highlight nuanced ideas. Cluster the content and connect it with arrows, connectors, and color. Use borders and bullets to relate ideas even further. For those who are ready for a "next step" of visual notetaking, have them consider balance and symmetry in their full-page sketch. How does it feel to them? Is it light, heavy, balanced?

Keep in mind that of course, some of your learners are ready for sketching independence and to craft with their own infinite creativity. Let them have at it! Some will need a boost to get started and a few probing questions to keep them on track, while still others will find tremendous value in you walking through the set up and modeling. An eye-opener for me is when I realize which of my participants are raring to go and which need support; it's fascinating how some learners are ready to roll in one given topic but crave support with another. Again, visual notes prevail with fresh insights into what drives participant learning and thinking.

To push those savvy thinkers in your class or meeting, ask them questions. *"How would the organization and hierarchy of your visual change from a different perspective or point of view? What else should be added to support the main idea? Where should the idea and important details connect? Would the emphasis need to shift? If so, why?"*

organizing ideas

Prominent title

NARWHALS

Supporting ICONS

WHITE SPACE
to add notes later
AND for
"BREATHING ROOM"

Connect,
Expand,
& Cluster
Information

Matching BULLETS
help connect ideas

CENTER the
ANCHORING PHENOMENON
or BIG IDEA

TIP: WATCH "HOW to DRAW" VIDEOS WITH YOUR STUDENTS
TO LEARN QUICKTIPS for DRAWING the ANCHOR IMAGE!

→ SIZE & SCALE
- CAPITAL LETTERS /
  LARGER LETTERS for
  MAIN IDEAS
- CREATES
  hierarchy
  of IDEAS

→ CLEAR CENTER
of GRAVITY

→ HIGHLIGHT COLOR
to make connections

→ DIFFERENT LINE WEIGHTS
thick vs. thin

WENDI PILLARS @Wendi322

—109—

Organization,
Part 2: Layouts & Templates

We could really get into the proverbial weeds here, but there are a handful of guidelines that help make a visual flow and make it easier for a viewer to follow.

Layouts are simply the way your information is laid out on the page or screen.

If unsure where to start, the scattered "popcorn" style is great for capturing ideas with no particular areas of importance or categories yet. This style is best for exploring information, ideas, or a vision, and are in a stage where the big takeaways or supporting details haven't been distinguished yet. Ideas are emerging as information is gathered.

Information can be written and collected on a single page, on sticky notes, or even on index cards. Using sticky notes and index cards makes it super easy to test what works without committing to a more deliberate visual. They are also ideal for eliciting ideas from your students or group members so that everyone is heard, and they can be added or set aside at any time.

Once you find patterns in your drawings and words, it's time to start putting them in clusters, a timeline, a flowchart, or whatever makes the most sense for the information. Here is where hierarchy, relevance, and more decision-making play a role. (Always decisions!)

Talk through and model the use of different layout styles as seen on the next page. Content will dictate style, and truth be told, with my participants I'm not always concerned about the notes following a certain pattern. Sometimes I just want them to be able to make connections, no matter where the information is on the page. If a particular layout is super important to the content (ie., cause and effect), then we walk through an outline together, so they know how it supports their understanding. I often model a basic set-up for page-sized visuals because I feel it jump-starts learners with positivity; I've discovered that one of the unexpected needs of doing this is that it helps emerging visual thinkers gauge spacing on their papers—including simply, *where* to start writing. Who knew?

Templates are another way to organize content. Akin to graphic organizers, these are handcrafted and designed for my audience at a given time, at a given ability level, with built-in scaffolds. They guide learners, ease anxiety of where to place things on the page, and are a quick formative assessment for me because I can easily see where the blank spaces are. As I mention later in the book about templates, they can be confining for the creatives, but they are effective in helping others figure out where to begin and how to filter through material.

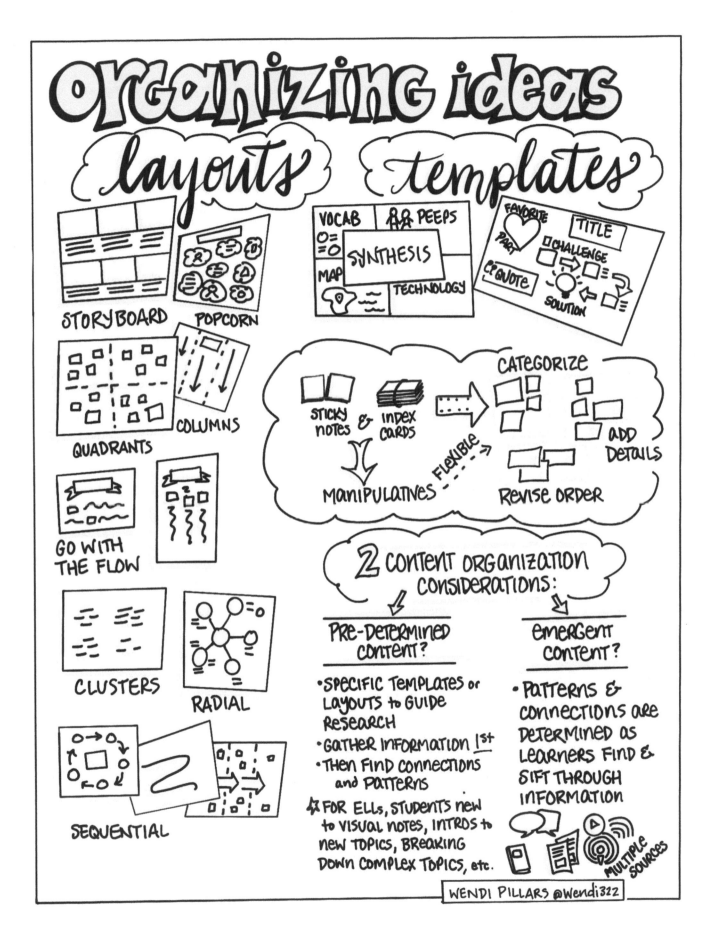

Organizing ideas

layouts

templates

STORYBOARD

POPCORN

VOCAB | PEEPS
SYNTHESIS
MAP | TECHNOLOGY

FAVORITE PART
TITLE
CHALLENGE
QUOTE
SOLUTION

QUADRANTS

COLUMNS

STICKY notes & INDEX cards → CATEGORIZE

MANIPULATIVES ‑‑‑ FLEXIBLE → REVISE ORDER

ADD DETAILS

GO WITH THE FLOW

CLUSTERS

RADIAL

2 Content organization considerations:

PRE-DETERMINED CONTENT?
- Specific templates or layouts to guide research
- Gather information 1st
- Then find connections and patterns
- ☆ For ELLs, students new to visual notes, intros to new topics, breaking down complex topics, etc.

EMERGENT CONTENT?
- Patterns & connections are determined as learners find & sift through information

MULTIPLE SOURCES

SEQUENTIAL

WENDI PILLARS @Wendi322

People

When I draw people, especially with learners, I admit I rely heavily on my stickman prowess. Granted, I tend toward a "fancier" boxy body style, but that's about as posh as I get. You can get a lot of mileage out of simple figures and it can be another teachable moment. Asking others to draw bodies in motion with mere stick figures is a mighty invitation to be more attentive on how our bodies move. Where are our arms when we run? How does our torso bend and where?

Using people, even the simplest figures, can also stimulate some unexpected, yet valuable, conversation. Social emotional awareness comes into play: how do you express a specific emotion using body language alone? Hunched shoulders, hanging head, long arms, and slightly bent knees definitely don't say "excited." Conversely, arms punched straight into the air, knees bent and lifted off the ground certainly can. What does "upset" look like and how is that different from "angry?" What kind of body language imparts messages for us? How can we draw that? (And notice, there was no mention of facial expression!)

As far as drawing faces, I rarely use faces when I'm drawing during a presentation unless it's pertinent. The audience can follow my lead or use faces if they want, but when I'm sketching quickly to explain something, I find that focusing on faces in general can be distracting for if they're not just right. These are ideas to keep in mind, and may or may not be the same in your context. When I do use them, I tend to exaggerate expressions just for fun. If you are interested in practicing more facial expressions, conduct an online search for how to draw faces in six steps for Austin Kleon's method using basic shapes.

One face drawing caveat—I DO use faces on objects quite a bit. A living document? Add a face. The Mother Earth? She deserves a face. Tree trunks, pencils, books, tacos, whatever you draw, when in doubt, anthropomorphize. Make objects into "people," because it's a lot of fun and they don't have to be as "perfect" as an actual face.

An issue I've faced more recently is how our sketches may perpetuate societal and social myths. Do we always portray secretaries as females and doctors as males? How do we address the implicit biases we all hold? What stereotypes might our drawings express, even if unintentionally? What alternatives can we mobilize with our markers? Will a simple black and white outline suffice, or does there need to be more nuanced color? How does the image we create influence the message we intend to send? What conversations do you need to have with marketing reps or learners along these lines? Why is this important, and what solutions are most fitting for your particular scenarios?

Photographs

Invite learners to sketch around photos or imagery to reveal their thinking using labels, icons, humor, annotations, connections, vocabulary words, and phrases. Imagine the ways you could use an activity like this to learn about each other as an autobiography at the start of a semester, as a running compendium of thinking and learning throughout a story, unit, or conference, or as part of a final assessment. Using photos adds an element of realism, a different level of relevance, and a chance to focus on connections and smaller details since the larger ideas are already provided visually. Photos assist audiences with inspiration and give permission to play a bit; since the pictures have done the heavy lift of representing ideas visually, learners can rely on their humor and personality to attach sketched icons and marks for emphasis.

Another simple idea is to pass a content-related photo around (or several if you have multiple groups or larger classes), and add phrases, words, and simple sketches to build on each other's knowledge. Participants examine and internalize others' ideas as they revisit information with new eyes, while gaining sketching ideas from peers.

In the language teaching world, a robust strategy for increasing vocabulary is the Picture Word Induction Model[12] (PWIM). The first step is for students to look at a content-related picture and to label actions, objects, people, places. Ideas can include what is visible and sometimes what is invisible but still has a role in the photo. (Maybe a time or date, climate and temperature, etc.) Together, teacher leading, the class first labels the photo, repeating the words and defining them. Instead of only words, try including small icons that could represent specific objects or actions, thereby building up your visual library for the upcoming lesson or unit. Subsequent lessons revisit the photo(s) and words using categorization, cloze activities, sentence-writing, and lastly, extended paragraph writing using those vocabulary words from day one. In addition to a written paragraph, modify the activity with students adding icons and symbols to create a storyboard.

One important note about grabbing non-personal photos or other images from the internet is that they must be credited. Please make it an explicit rule for your learners; if it's not a photo you took, find out who did and give them credit.

What else can you think of? What could this look like in your meeting, training, or classroom?

AUTADIDACT

VISUAL NOTE-TAKING FOR EDUCATORS

AUTHOR

BASEBALL FAN

MOM

OVERSEAS & BACK AGAIN

MILITARY & CIVILIAN

NORTH CAROLINA

OHIO

BEEKEEPER

GROSVENOR TEACHER FELLOW

Ridiculous MOM

"I'M TOO COOL" Teenager

LOVER of MAPS (CHARTS!)

Wendi Pillars

Planning Lessons or Presentations

The next page is pretty text-heavy, but you can see that information is actually clearly chunked and categorized to make it easier to read. The main point to remember is that visual notes are about so much more than "drawing pictures" and can be integrated in numerous ways with varied purposes and outcomes. Just look at all the thought that goes into visual notes AND how they can be used. This is a list you can share with colleagues unfamiliar with the benefits of visual notes.

In the visual, note that main ideas are written with hierarchy—larger and in bold, and are farther set apart by a thin box around each title. Bullet point phrases are written in smaller lowercase letters. The small bullets are the same design within categories but differ among them, such as stars, little people, squares, or circles. One simple sketch accompanies each category.

How could you use this style as a stepping stone for your audience and how they in turn present information? How can they visually distinguish main ideas from details? Set apart topics? Add simple imagery? Categorize information differently? What would you like to see when your participants and learners are showing what they know? How can you then take them to the next level and guide them to connect information and organize it in new or different ways?

Planning lessons:
— WHAT to CONSIDER —
(It's about so much more than "drawing pictures.")

OBJECTIVES:

- Why do you want to use vis notes?
- How will they help connect particularly important points?
- Where are good stopping points in your lesson for formative checks?
- What type of information should students understand, listen, look for?
- What will students <u>do</u> with the notes?

EXPECTATIONS:

- Will you grade the notes?
- Specific content or presentation expectations?
- Legibility: typography, hierarchy
- Tangible connections, invisible connections
- Novel thought, originality
- Artistic representation
- Humor
- Specific vocabulary use
- Minimum connections expected
- Big ideas vs. important details
- Precise purpose of sketch: one-time or base for adding subsequent details
- <u>Medium</u> for sketching: pencils erase, but markers do not ⟹ increased ownership
- Analog vs. digital: which suits your needs and objectives best?

AUDIENCE:

- Who will be using, seeing the notes?
- Will subsequent drafts be shared?
- Will they be hung up for peers to see or posted online somewhere?

STANDARDS:

Standards
1.2
1.2a
2.3

- Analyzing ideas
- Finding evidence to support a claim
- Finding main ideas & details
- Discovering, highlighting, emphasizing relationships
- Using new vocabulary in context
- Summarizing and synthesizing, from picture books to AP texts and more
- Interpreting word meanings, both literal and figurative
- Trace and evaluate lines of thinking and reasoning
- Chunking and categorizing evidence for arguments or supporting claims
- Use visuals to clarify findings and emphasize salient points

ETCETERA...

WENDI PILLARS @WENDI322

—117—

Practical Pedagogy

When we think about what works in class or training, there are a few questions to keep in mind. The number one question we should be asking is what our purpose is, what we want students to walk away knowing *today*. It's easy to get overwhelmed, but breaking it down into the essence, stripping the content down of its fluff first, can help you see more clearly. It's not about what activity looks fun to do; it's about what activity will help promote the learning you want to see.

So, what makes sense for your learners, with this content, at this time? Why?

How can you show the big picture *and* the parts that make up the whole? How can you push beyond rote recall and into answers and understanding they can apply in other scenarios besides on a routine test? How can you incorporate their voices into the learning? How will you harvest feedback from your audience about their learning and about the classroom community? How will you optimize this content to foster better community among your learners?

I believe there will always be more questions than answers, but if you're clear on what your current audience needs most to succeed, with your content, at this time, then that's a pretty solid pedagogical foundation.

PRACTICAL PEDAGOGY

WHAT'S YOUR PURPOSE?

WHAT ARE ONE OR TWO IDEAS YOU WANT STUDENTS TO WALK AWAY WITH <u>TODAY</u>?

ZOOM IN ON YOUR MESSAGE.

PLANNING

WHAT MAKES the MOST SENSE for YOUR LEARNERS and YOUR CONTENT AT THIS TIME?

PUSH STUDENTS to THINK DEEPLY

- SEE the WHOLE PICTURE & its PARTS
- HELP STUDENTS DEVELOP CONCRETE IDEAS to TAKE ACTION
- BALANCE STUDENT IDEAS & VOICE with NEW INSIGHTS FROM YOU
- PUSH BEYOND STUDENTS' SIMPLE ANSWERS about how they can IMPACT & CHANGE the WORLD.

BUILD RELATIONSHIPS

- MIRRORS·
- WINDOWS·
- BRIDGES·

Process Over Pretty

I cannot say enough about this, fellow visual thinkers. The process of creating visual notes is exceptionally rich with treasures. I have been humbled many times by assuming I "knew" what my learners were thinking, where their understanding lay, and any misconceptions they held during. Boy, have I been wrong.

Academically, through the use of visual notetaking, tiny little facts have resurfaced that my learners recalled to make stunning connections to what we were learning later. And I thought they weren't listening! Personally, I've learned about home lives, family histories, and emotions that impacted their interpretation of a poem or text and made me see material through entirely new lenses. I've seen adults and students alike positively explode with animation when asked to explain what appeared to be an indiscriminate set of lines, but yet for them was a sketch abundant with nuance and meaning far beyond what they would have been capable of writing in words. Or in a single minute time limit. I've been stopped in my tracks by realizations of patterns I see among certain learners' drawings, forcing me to rethink my norms with utter humility. In my decades of using visual notes, there hasn't been a single age group immune to their potential to promote deeper understanding and personal expression.

In short, the process of my students taking visual notes has opened up incredible windows into their lives. This in turn has helped me teach, facilitate, and present content more effectively in myriad situations. Talk about unexpected gifts of stick men and simple icons.

In case you or your particular audience get stuck during the process of representing information visually, do what I do:

Draw horribly. Laugh at yourself.

Your audience will laugh and make fun of your drawings and tell you they can do so much better. Give them the marker and plenty of permission to have at it. Once they manifest their sketch, then talk about connections, labels, any extra details needed, and more. And just know that (knock on wood) I've always been able to get "unstuck" when taking notes in class or group settings thanks to others' ingenuity. Give your learners or group members the benefit of the doubt and always remind them to "make it POP!" (Not quite grammatically correct if you spell it out, but hey, it's quicker to say than "process over pretty.")

Come to think of it, "process over pretty" is actually a pretty good mantra for life. Planning, thinking, revising, revisiting, and reflecting, all in the name of learning and laughing a little bit more.

Questions to Ask

Number one: ***"How can we represent that with a visual?"*** This is my go-to question for all ages and all audiences. I know it's working when I hear learners ask this of each other.

Number two: ***"Tell me about your sketch/visual."*** (Okay, not a question, per se, but you're seeking information.) NEVER judge someone's "art" or visual representation. I can't tell you how many times I have been simultaneously humbled and amazed at learner ingenuity. I've learned that what might look like more of a scribble has held vast insight and understanding which I never would have seen had I asked those same people to express themselves in writing or had I not slowed down in the first place. Seeing how others choose to represent content visually is like a treasure box—you never know what you might find, but you must be open!

As far as pre-planning questions, consider where good stopping points are in your lesson, presentation, or learning material. Where are the key words, concepts, and ideas? When should they be pulled together? And how about that critical brain break? Stop talking for a couple of minutes to let your audience think through their learning and provide you with a rapid formative assessment or maybe even a brief summary. It may be humbling, but definitely worthwhile.

On the next page you'll see some questions I commonly ask and which our participants should learn to ask each other. What other questions can you add?

How can we represent that with a visual?

★ WHAT ARE GOOD STOPPING POINTS?
- KEY WORDS, CONCEPTS, IDEAS
- BRAIN BREAK (EVERY 10-15 MINUTES!)
- QUICK FORMATIVE ASSESSMENTS
- BRIEF SUMMARIES

NEVER JUDGE A STUDENT'S "ART." FOCUS ON THE THINKING PROCESS.

★ PRE-PLAN QUESTIONS & COMMENTS:

★★★ TELL ME ABOUT YOUR SKETCH / VISUAL

WHAT DO THESE DETAILS REPRESENT?

WHY DID YOU CHOOSE/ PRIORITIZE THESE DETAILS?

☺ TELL ME MORE

WHAT ARE YOU MOST EXCITED ABOUT/ PROUD OF IN YOUR VISUAL?

WHAT DETAILS COULD YOU ADD TO HIGHLIGHT X,Y,Z ?

WHAT IS ONE MORE DETAIL YOU COULD ADD TO DISTINGUISH CHARACTER/ PLACE IDEA "A" FROM "B"?

COMPARE & CONTRAST YOUR VISUAL WITH A PARTNER'S. ADD AT LEAST ONE NEW DETAIL.

WHAT IDEAS CAN YOU ADD ?

WENDI PILLARS @Wendi322

 Quotes

One of the things I love most about reading is analyzing how authors put their words together, how brilliantly a symphony of ideas can be expressed through the alchemy of wordsmithing. I try to teach participants and learners to keep track of phrases or even sentences that they like as they read, or hear in a video or podcast.

"Like" is such a subjective concept: maybe a phrase resonates in a deeply personal way because of prior experience or something more recent; maybe it evokes a strong emotion—either positive or negative; maybe, just maybe it reminds them of something else, a friend, a song, or an activity they were doing the last time they heard the word. Maybe it can relate to an organization or business for marketing; or maybe it's a way to tangibly gauge what your audience is actually "hearing" or interpreting.

The point is for our audiences to become more aware of the nuances that help build a story and to heighten their word awareness while reading and listening to speakers. One way to do this is to have them sketch a quote or key phrases from a story or text, or during a meeting. These sketches can then be displayed much like a word wall for everyone to see, serving as a shared reference and recall aid for that particular context. Sketching a quote can focus on different lettering styles alone and their corresponding aura or they can include imagery. Can they select colors that evoke the tone of the quote or the context itself? Challenge visual thinkers to represent a scene or famous quote with images alone as a game. Finding ways to increase attention to words and the intention to remember are the foremost goals.

Visual notetaking, even if the notes are word-centric with few images, always serves as an opportunity to "sit" with the content a bit more and to view it from different angles. It's a way for to consider tone, key ideas, important ideas for themselves *at that time*, while serving as a physical artifact they can use to measure how thinking has evolved over time.

SKETCH a QUOTE
or KEY PHRASES

FROM
- FICTION
- POETRY
- NON-FICTION
- PRIMARY SOURCES
- MULTIMEDIA SOURCES
- GUEST SPEAKERS
- FIELD TRIPS
- PEER QUOTES
- REFLECTIONS
- SHARED EXPERIENCES
- CURRENT EVENTS
  and more...

EMPHASIZE Key words with BOLD letters, size, capital letters, color, etc.

CATEGORIZE related ideas with color and font

SHARE & JUSTIFY which words did you choose and why?

DISPLAY throughout unit for additional means of recall

NOTABLY HEIGHTENS ATTENTION DURING READING

⭐ Which words truly resonate with me?

⭐ What are important ideas I want to remember?

⭐ What are Key ideas according to the author?

⭐ How can I represent these words in a sketch?

⭐ What container would work for this content/mood?

⭐ What colors and font "fit"/match the tone?

PROMOTES: close reading & listening | critical thinking | personal expression | time to "sit" with content | classroom community

WENDI PILLARS @WENDI322

Reading,
Part 1: All Phases of Reading

Many people enjoy reading, but I feel it's safe to say that many also lack the confidence in their own reading abilities. With this in mind, it's beneficial to remember our brain's penchant for visualizing, and how natural it can be as a default strategy and a comprehension tool to rely upon. A large chunk of primate brains is devoted to vision, about thirty or so areas within the occipital, temporal, and parietal lobes. Reading, and even more importantly, re-reading with all of their inherent requirements for success, are two activities that optimize these powers of visual thinking.

Visual thinkers can sketch during all phases of reading, from the pre-reading phase with predictions or dives into their background knowledge. They can sketch while reading, after reading, and during re-reading at a later time. Other skills can come into play such as comparing and contrasting sketches and interpretations with one another, writing questions to extend text exploration, and reflecting on how thinking has shifted with the onset of new knowledge.

Learners can take on a different role or perspective for their sketching which can inspire some interesting dialogue later. Encourage them to use their notes as supporting documents and anchors for their arguments, presentations, and general responses.

Create visuals to go with vocabulary words and build a living word wall. This is for elementary students through adults! All learners benefit from word-building and heightened word awareness. Post words in the classroom, and if you are a travelling teacher, affix them to a piece of butcher block paper or chart paper to carry with you. Dividing and conquering a potentially daunting word list from, say, a novel, and assigning words among the class can be a lot more doable. It holds learners accountable in a different way if they're the only one responsible for their word because they know others are relying upon their work.

Another hook for all learners is teaching how to draw a main character or a main element of a story or nonfiction text. It empowers them, especially when you draw it along with them. Not sure how? Watch a how-to draw video together or borrow a how-to draw book from the library. Double bonus comes from your time modeling how to learn something new and the fact they can still learn something cool from books. (She says in her least biased voice.)

Working in an organization? What are some common phrases, symbols, and key words that highlight the strengths and favorite attributes of your service or product that others might read about? Are there key elements that team members could learn to draw or create to better message your business to others on the fly? Posting these creative ideas publicly can encourage team members to be creative and to internalize them.

> "An hour spent reading is one stolen from paradise."
>
> —THOMAS WARTON

reading

✏️ SKETCH during pre-reading (PREDICT), during reading, post-reading, and re-reading

✏️ COMPARE & CONTRAST pre- and post-reading sketches

What new knowledge was gained?

Which details became more important?

How has your thinking shifted?

▶️ TEACH STUDENTS HOW to DRAW a MAIN CHARACTER or ELEMENT from the TEXT

learn together!

SKETCH from DIFFERING PERSPECTIVES

• SKETCH CRITICAL VOCABULARY & DISPLAY on WALLS, ABOVE the BOARD, ETC. for easy VISIBILITY (yes, even in high schools!)

• SHARE a CLASSROOM? AFFIX VOCAB SKETCHES to CHART PAPER for PORTABILITY

WENDI PILLARS @ WENDI 322

Reading,
Part 2: Revisiting & Interacting with Notes

I mentioned re-reading on the first page which we all know is critical for comprehension. Oftentimes educators provide fresh purposes for learners to dig back into a text, to put eyes on it again, in search of more evidence. We need learners to do the same with their notes. We ask them to "take notes," but what's the value of them if they aren't revisited and reviewed? With visual notes, there is a greater tendency and willingness to step back in and *do something* with what they've created. (Even using the word "created" vs "written" shows that these notes are different.) Leaders and facilitators can ask participants to categorize ideas and imagery after a day or two. What connections have they discovered since initially taking the notes? What details can they now add or revise? Keep questioning to hold learners accountable for their own thinking, and critically, how it has shifted and grown since gaining new knowledge.

Categorizing is a powerful thinking strategy. Use closed and open sorts to represent relationships from unique angles. In a closed sort, you would provide the category, with your audience determining which words, imagery, and other evidence fit into that category. They would then explain their choices and how they relate.

In an open sort, you will see what categories emerge from a given set of facts, a text, or other evidence based on learner perspective. Participants need to justify the relationships within each category, which is just a lot of fun because you can quickly see how creative your visual thinkers can be, even in emergent stages! They won't even notice that they've been dipping back into their notes and the text for ideas.

Many reading strategies lend themselves to using added imagery. Try a modified jigsaw activity with the audience reading their respective parts of a text and creating visuals to accompany written or oral summaries. They then share their visual summaries, along with the thinking behind the visuals they created. Extend learning by asking them to share not only their thinking process, but maybe their sketching process—can they teach others how they created their sketch or a single element of it? As a teacher or organizational leader, be on the lookout for unique imagery portrayals, even if one tiny part of a whole visual. Ask participants one on one if they'd be willing to share how they drew something or how they came up with such a unique idea, then watch their confidence soar.

reading

REVISIT NOTES WITH a PURPOSE

DEEPEN understanding
- CATEGORIZE sentences/ideas
- Make EXPLICIT connections
- Re-read text to ADD details

MODIFIED JIGSAW

- READ assigned text
- CREATE visuals to accompany written or oral summaries
- SHARE summaries & thinking behind visuals
- Students TEACH EACH OTHER how to draw/replicate sketches
- Use SHARED DETAILS to recreate the text

HOW DO IDEAS relate?

Categorize, then title each to represent how the information relates.

CLOSED SORT	OPEN SORT
provide categories	allow categories to emerge
students find information	justify word relationships

Yet another purpose to RE-READ for Key ideas and to THINK CRITICALLY!

 WHAT IDEAS can you add?

Reading,
Part 3: Small Steps to Get Started

If you're not sure where to start, take it step by step, page by page, or stanza by stanza with quick sketches in the margins. Tiny sketches don't seem as daunting for learners, and they tend to be faster if you're worried about time. Have sticky notes on hand for learners to use, and color code if you want: one color for vocabulary, one for content, for example.

Sketching out key vocabulary is always important which is why it's been mentioned on all three reading pages. As a current high school teacher, I'd love to see greater learner confidence in using more descriptive vocabulary, so we look for figurative language, metaphors, and polysemous words (those words with multiple meanings like "table") to highlight and distinguish. In my experience, once students sketch a few of these, they relax into it, having realized that this kind of word play isn't so bad after all.

Vocabulary and shared language within a business organization is also critical. Different teams may use different terminology; if your goals relate to increasing clear communication, have teams create a visual vocabulary to share so that reading any notifications or updates is unambiguous. This is also an effective practice for new hires who may need to learn the lingo quickly.

Another favorite tool to use is a wordless book. I know this is a "reading" page, but oh, the resonance and richness of pages that tell a story without words! Viewers can interpret what is happening in fiction and nonfiction texts, then summarize with visual notes that combine both words and pictures. Use wordless books or a series of pictures/photos that relate directly to your content, ask them to integrate specific vocabulary perhaps, and see what their imaginations devise. Use a couple of pictures from the book, and have learners fill in the rest before comparing and contrasting with the actual story. Base predictions on the first two to three pages. Do this as a pre-assessment for a unit, during a unit, or as a post-assessment, and guide students to self-assess their growth in more nuanced understanding.

Analysis of how imagery is non-linear in telling a story helps visual thinkers reflect upon how pictures can be interpreted much more broadly than pure text. How will that impact marketing mindsets and visual communication practices?

reading

📑 SKETCH DURING FIRST READ of COMPLEX TEXT USING TITLE, HEADINGS, VOCABULARY, etc.

Sticky notes for smaller sketches OR a larger surface for a record of evolving understanding

📑 SKETCH BY PAGE, STANZA, SECTION, PHRASES and KEY TERMS as ONGOING COMPREHENSION ASSESSMENT

📑 TRY SKETCHING FIGURATIVE LANGUAGE, METAPHORS, WORD PLAY, NUANCES, POLYSEMOUS WORDS

She was a couch potato in the gravy boat of life...

📑 SKETCH WORDLESS SUMMARIES of NONFICTION or FICTION TEXTS

WENDI PILLARS @WENDI32Z

—131—

Speaking,
Part 1: Use Sketches as an Anchor

I have four sketched pages dedicated to speaking, and although many of the ideas may seem obvious and simple, they are critical ideas for well-rounded, memorable learning. Shifting the ratio of presenter to audience talk requires intentional planning and an understanding that oral language supports all other forms of literacy.

My primary job is helping students acquire English as another language, so I place exponentially more effort engaging students in speaking during class than a typical content teacher might. This bleeds over into my presentation style, as well, with intention to be interactive. One sobering commonality among my newcomer students and many who aren't yet proficient in English, is that they don't speak in their other classes throughout the day. Not with partners, not answering questions, not having discussions in class. Nothing.

Wow. Shockingly, this occurs similarly in board meetings among professional, paid adults.

That's so hard for me to hear and it galvanizes me to work harder to incorporate some type of speaking activity within my instructional routines on a consistent basis, and to share what works with colleagues. Visual notes, even the smallest ones, have such power to draw in an audience while boosting confidence for the speaker. In the language acquisition world, having an object for learners to focus on while they are practicing their oral skills lowers their affective filter, meaning that they're more comfortable and less afraid to speak. Sometimes, as much as we expect it in an American setting, eye contact can be incredibly intimidating and focusing instead on a sketch they've created, for example, with occasional eye contact can ease anxieties.

Consider the benefits of visual notes with your non-native English speakers, your shy team members, and your "helium hand" audience members who are always the first to answer. If the audience can sit with their thoughts and sketch them out for two to three minutes, EVERYONE gets a chance to think and respond. Your highfliers can add nuance and become curious to hear about what others know. With that extra bit of time to process, all participants will be more prepared to talk about their thinking especially if they can use their sketch as an anchor to point to and look at while speaking. You'll be a Wait Time Champion, and the opportunities for conversation might expand with your audience's increased preparation.

Another oracy component is to have participants describe their visual, demonstrate how they may have drawn a certain image, or conduct a think aloud for others to go behind the scenes in their mind. These speaking sessions can be in small groups, with partners, or in front of everyone. They can even be recorded speaking individually for practice. Provide sentence frames to support more precise and academic conversational competence. Even small bursts of practice help build much needed self-confidence and helps everyone feel heard, while small groups ensure that more than one person is processing information and remembering at a time.

Speaking:

🗨️ HAVE STUDENTS DESCRIBE, EXPLAIN, AND/OR JUSTIFY THEIR SKETCHES & SKETCH ELEMENTS

Tell me more about why you chose to represent X with Y.

How did you prioritize which fact /detail /event/ person to include in your visual?

Tell 🏰 more about your visual.

🗨️ HAVE STUDENTS DEMONSTRATE & EXPLAIN THEIR LETTERING, SKETCHING, AND/OR THINKING PROCESS

→ BOOSTS METACOGNITION & REFLECTION

PARTNERS

SMALL GROUPS

WHOLE CLASS

DIGITALLY

WENDI PILLARS @Wendi322

—133—

Speaking,
Part 2: Find More Opportunities for Speaking

It's really tough to extract the skills of listening from the skills of speaking. I mean, really, what's the use of good speaking if no one is listening? Part of the purpose behind speaking is to be compelling, and one simple way is to include a visual.

When we teach others about creating presentations and the purposes behind them, we also need to demonstrate and practice different levels of questioning. In my experience, I've noticed it is imperative to provide support through sentence frames and question starters. This works for all levels, especially when processing new information. It's commonly stated that ALL learners are academic language learners; we can't expect them to properly express academic and technical language through osmosis. It has to be taught and practiced with intention.

As we teach and lead, I believe we should also be teaching our audiences about how their brain learns, explain the strategies we are using and ask learners to evaluate and reflect upon how, or if, particular strategies work for them or why they don't. The same with Bloom's questioning taxonomy. We have to show learners how to ask different levels of questions and let them experience the hierarchy of responses that come with diverse types of inquiry. This is not only for content, but also for feedback on each other's work. Model appropriate responses. Ask multiple levels of questions about a learner's sketch, and expect that their responses are based on evidence in their sketch. You get the idea.

Visual thinkers can learn to respond to different types of questions using supportive academic frameworks and vocabulary, but it takes time and it doesn't end there. Aim for learners to be able to ask higher level questions with varying levels of support. We want them to be able to ASK and ANSWER questions, to respond thoughtfully to diverse perspectives and ideas that someone else is articulating or disclosing. We want them to go beyond "What is that?" when encountering a new image or idea, and to be able to question something new with expressive detail. Peer feedback can be a game-changer: let's make sure it's productive and constructive.

Too often our spoken presentations and conversational discourse levels are far from where we need them to be. Visual notes help with focus, recall, questioning practice, and serve as an anchor for precise, confident academic or technical language use. Combine talking with written language; both are "productive" skills, meaning they require linguistic output from the students. We will never know what our audience is learning until they produce something for feedback.

How often do you provide opportunities for your audiences to show what they know each day or during each meeting? More importantly, how can you add more opportunities?

Speaking:

TAKE TIME TO TEACH STUDENTS ABOUT DIFFERENT LEVELS OF QUESTIONING. IT PREVENTS THEM FROM RELYING ON "WHAT IS THAT?" AS THEY LEARN TO INQUIRE ABOUT OTHERS' WORK AND THINKING.

Practice academic language

Persuade

Argue

Inform

PURPOSES

Question

Narrate

Sketches help with FOCUS and RECALL

PROVIDE SENTENCE FRAMES & QUESTION STEMS FROM BLOOM'S TAXONOMY OR A SIMILAR QUESTIONING HIERARCHY.

EXAMPLES:
- Why is _____ significant?
- How is _____ an example of _____?
- Re-tell _____ in your own words.
- What ideas can you add to _____?
- What might happen if you combined _____ with _____?
- Do you agree that _____? Explain.
- What criteria would you use to assess _____?

RESPOND THOUGHTFULLY TO DIVERSE PERSPECTIVES. VISUAL NOTES CAN BE AN INCREDIBLE WINDOW INTO OTHERS' THINKING.

SPEAKING PROVIDES INSIGHTS!

PERSPECTIVES... MATTER....

WENDI PILLARS @Wendi322

Speaking,
Part 3: Level Up Presentations

Presentations. Whew. A loaded concept in the academic world. Or the business world for that matter. They can be simple, but we definitely want to steer speakers and presenters away from pure reliance on Google Slides or PowerPoint.

Part of successful presentations and speaking opportunities depends on audience participation and reaction, and it's no different in the boardroom or the classroom. Speaking and holding academic and technically precise conversations is challenging for many, especially language learners or those unfamiliar with occupation-specific terminology. Listeners have a lot to hold in their minds as they interpret what others are saying, formulate and translate their own responses or questions, and actually drum up the courage to spit it out. Boardroom and classroom community are vital and non-negotiable, one borne of respect for each person and their abilities, otherwise these golden opportunities for learning will be lost.

A supreme gift of sketches is that whether super simple or intricately complex, they can be enhanced with oral explanations. Participants can not only describe and explain their work, but they can use the opportunity to justify their many decisions, while peers analyze, evaluate, and practice asking clarifying questions and negotiating deeper meanings. This permits everyone the chance to demonstrate their understanding and thinking at numerous levels.

While we're talking about different levels, a good reminder is to never discount simplicity. Sometimes the simplest sketch comes from a wealth of background knowledge begging for an outlet. Speakers can convey their knowledge and experiences or even try to persuade others to view their visual notes as *they* intended. (Some of the sketches are quick draws without much detail, so those become ideal vehicles for more extended oral explanation.) Speakers can promote arguments or highlight humor using drawings to expand details.

Practicing a mix of open-ended and closed-ended questions is ideal. Closed questions are ones that can be answered with a simple "yes" or "no" or in-the-text questions like "what is the goal of our team?" with a very limited set of answers. These are perfect for your newest team members and emerging language learners because they still invite participation, scaffolded for their ability and knowledge levels. Open questions allow for anything beyond yes, no, or limited information answers. As another support, you can provide questions to participants ahead of time so they can prepare and practice responses about their own visual notes with confidence. You can choose one or two specific questions or encourage learners to create their own.

So many ideas. What are yours?

Speaking: & Questioning

BUILD A COMMUNITY OF TRUST AND LEVERAGE THAT TO CLARIFY, VERIFY OR CHALLENGE IDEAS, INFERENCES, OR CONCLUSIONS.

► MONITOR DURING SKETCHING
► MODEL QUESTIONING & CURIOSITY

BOTH THE SIMPLEST AND THE MORE COMPLEX SKETCHES CAN BE ENHANCED WITH ORAL EXPLANATIONS.

STUDENTS CREATE FORMAL PRESENTATIONS THAT INCLUDE THEIR SKETCH(ES). (TOOLS CAN INCLUDE PREZI, VIDEO, SLIDES, OR ON PAPER/WHITEBOARD, ETC.)

AUDIENCE/PEERS CAN DEVELOP & ASK QUESTIONS OF EACH OTHER. (ORAL PRACTICE FOR EVERYONE!)

 • OPEN  and CLOSED QUESTIONS

make them THINK

- HOW DOES ___ CONNECT WITH WHAT WE LEARNED BEFORE?
- WHY IS _____ IMPORTANT?
- WHAT ARE SOME POSSIBLE DETAILS WE CAN ADD TO OUR SKETCHES?
- WHAT IS THE MEANING OF ____?

- HOW WOULD YOUR SKETCH CHANGE IF YOU INCLUDED INFORMATION FROM __?
- WHAT WOULD YOU ELIMINATE IF YOUR SKETCH COULD ONLY FIT ON AN INDEX CARD?
- WHAT MISUNDERSTANDINGS SHOULD YOUR AUDIENCE BE AWARE OF?

WENDI PILLARS @Wendi322

Speaking,
Part 4: Collaborative Sketching

Whenever we focus on students' oral language development, it improves their reading ability, as far as both fluency and comprehension. When their reading ability improves, so does their writing. The ones having focused conversations in class, whether persuading, arguing, informing, justifying, questioning, or narrating are the ones doing the thinking. If they're doing the thinking, then guess what? They're doing the learning. It's true: deeper thinking *can* absolutely begin with a visual note which is discussed orally in small groups, with partners, or among the whole group.

If you're looking for more ideas to encourage conversation while sketching, try collaborative visual note-taking. Team members can use this time to review and summarize different units, lessons, or parts of lessons; once the visuals are complete, hang them up for a gallery walk. Conversations during creation can be exceptionally rich when "no one" is listening. Circulate through the room, though, and you'll hear snippets of questions that will make your heart burst. "What images would best represent this topic?" "What is the background knowledge of our audience?" "Which details would make the most sense in this space we have left?," "No, this would make more sense over here, next to this fact," and more.

A display like a gallery walk (you can always commandeer the hallway if there's not enough space in your area) can be time for participants to devise leveled questions in writing and provide specific, constructive feedback according to norms and expectations you've established.

If you're working with a larger group, learners can also upload them into Google Slides or another digital platform with a voiced narration so that others can view and listen later with the ability to pause as needed.

In case you haven't noticed, visual notes fit pretty seamlessly into most activities you might already do in your meetings, workshops, presentations, and classes and there aren't any limits that I'm aware of as to *how* you can expand their use. Whether using bite-size visual notes or larger ones, as long as your content is increasingly understandable, memorable, shareable, and fun, then you're on the right path.

Speaking:

OTHERS' IDEAS AND INTERPRETATIONS HELP BUILD & DEEPEN UNDERSTANDING.

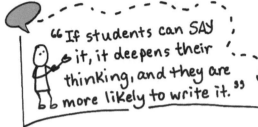
" If students can SAY it, it deepens their thinking, and they are more likely to write it. "

THIS NECESSARILY REQUIRES DEVELOPED LISTENING SKILLS!

USING SKETCHES AS FOCAL POINT REDUCES ANXIETY & PROMOTES DISCUSSION

COLLABORATIVE SKETCHING ENCOURAGES VERBAL SIFTING THROUGH IDEAS. IT'S A JOY TO LISTEN TO CONVERSATIONS AND QUESTIONS LIKE THIS HAPPEN NATURALLY.

What is the background knowledge of our audience?

What images would best represent this topic?

What do you think we are missing?

What are the main ideas we need to incorporate?

What is the focal point of our visual?

Are there cultural aspects we should consider?

Which colors best represent the tone of our topic?

★ OF COURSE, POSTING QUESTIONS LIKE THESE FOR STUDENTS TO GUIDE THEIR THINKING IS AN IDEAL SCAFFOLD.

WENDI PILLARS @Wendi322

—139—

Speech Bubbles

Akin to borders (containers), speech bubbles can add a little panache to quotes, words that resonate, dialogue, pivotal events, and central ideas. Again, these are simple shapes to draw with no set rules while employing a gentle kick-start for the imagination.

How can the shape of the speech bubble highlight or emphasize the tone of the text? Is it whimsical? Humorous? Somber? Tight-laced or regimented? Are the thoughts definitive or an inkling of possibility? Action-oriented or reflective?

Challenge your visual thinkers to make a shape that somehow represents the context or topic. Birds? Balloons? Ideas? Ocean waves? Clouds? Clothing? People? Historical artifacts? Surprises? WWII technology? Marketing concepts? Organizational changes? Will it need thick dark lines or thin, dashed lines to set it off? Can you cluster like bubbles or create contrasting elements?

How creative can you be?

*Note: Write your words FIRST, then draw the speech bubble or border around them so they don't get squished!

"SAY WHAT?"

IDEAS for USE
- CENTRAL IDEA(S)
- DIALOGUE
- POWERFUL QUOTES
- WORDS/PHRASES THAT RESONATE
- PIVOTAL DETAILS/EVENTS
- SHAPE CAN HIGHLIGHT/EMPHASIZE TONE
- SHAPE CAN REPRESENT CONTEXT/TOPIC

WENDI PILLARS @Wendi322

Technology

Full disclosure. Yes, I really like my iPad, but at heart I am an analog girl. Give me a marker or a pen any day and I'd be happy. That being said, here are my top digital sketching suggestions with the full realization that tech updates occur fast enough to make your head spin. By the time this goes to print, who knows what new apps, bells, and whistles will grace our workflow.

My time-honored go-to has been Procreate ($) for the iPad. I've used it for years now, and am simply used to it. I love the multiple layers, the ability to record time-lapse videos, to project my work, and the ability to illustrate nuanced pieces of work. I'm currently learning to use Concepts which I appreciate for its infinite screen and vector capabilities.

I used to rely on Sketchbook Pro by Autodesk, (now free and for Android) which is what I used extensively back in the day with my free stylus that was on the tip of a free pen I received at a conference. Which is to say, I had the iPad that simply said "iPad," and still created some pretty impactful sketches with a far-from-fancy stylus. One word of caution, though. My iPad "disappeared" while I had it at school one day, and I never did find it or—heartbreakingly—my years of sketches compiled within. I eventually purchased the iPad pro, eager to download my Sketchbook app, only to realize that there was now only a new version of the app and the old app could no longer be accessed. Talk about crushed. (And yes, I tried borrowing older iPads to try downloading, to no avail . . .) Lesson learned: if your sketches mean anything to you, **back them up somewhere**, and don't rely completely on your app to house them.

Paper by WeTransfer is intuitive, and it's free but you can pay a few dollars to upgrade your brush selection. Sketches are all stored in digital "sketchbooks" within the app, which obviously helps a bunch with organization.

Inkflow and Adobe Illustrator Draw (both for Android, too), Tayasui Sketches and Educreations are still in my toolbox, but again, I can do all that I need to (so far!) in Procreate. Educreations now charges a fee to upgrade, and at this point it's not worth it for me. I've also dabbled with Explain Everything which is pretty popular and intuitive to use.

Another app, highlighted on the next page, is Notability which is now also a paid app. It transforms hand-written notes to text, records sound and narrated video as you sketch or talk about your notes, scans documents as pdfs and lets you write on other pdfs like a boss. I really the continuous vertical scroll, so you can just keep writing without having to go out and snag another page then start again. It's pretty quick and easy to use, and you can easily share your work. I don't use it for nuanced work, but otherwise it is a pretty powerful notetaking tool.

If I had to suggest one paid app, it would be Procreate. Notability would come in a close second. I understand that GoodNotes ($) is a strong competitor for Notability, but I've not tried it. I'm also an Apple Pencil convert, but still tend to carry old pens topped with a stylus just in case, and I've recently covered my iPad screen with the Paperlike matte screen protector which gives my pencil a little more traction.

TECHNOLOGY

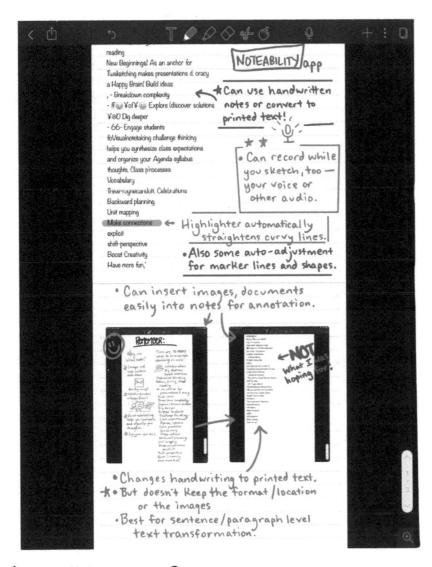

NOTEABILITY app

*Can use handwritten notes or convert to printed text!

• Can record while you sketch, too — your voice or other audio.

Highlighter automatically straightens curvy lines.
• Also some auto-adjustment for marker lines and shapes.

• Can insert images, documents easily into notes for annotation.

→ NOT what I was hoping for!

• Changes handwriting to printed text.
*• But doesn't keep the format/location or the images
• Best for sentence/paragraph level text transformation.

FAVORITE APP:
PROCREATE

• LAYERS
• ease of use
• MYRIAD BRUSHES
• IMPORT MATERIAL
• EXPORT as JPEG, PDF, TIME-LAPSE VIDEO
• MORE NUANCED WORK/ART
• easy to SHARE

☆ PRESENT your work through AIRPLAY & SCREEN MIRRORING.

KEEP it SIMPLE.

☆ REMEMBER YOUR OBJECTIVES
☆ FOR LEARNING. SKETCHING AND DEEPER THINKING DO NOT DEPEND ON a DIGITAL PLATFORM.

WENDI PILLARS @WENDI322

Templates

The next few pages have lesson plan templates (more in the Appendices) to spark ideas and help you organize your planning information. Some are designed for teachers while others were created to share with participants and learners. Again, any way that we can make learning objectives clearer is a bonus for our audiences. Here are some pros and cons to using templates:

Pros: Based on my experience, there is a greater drive for users to complete the work, to find all the "pieces" to fill in with a given template. Having specific purposes to dig back into a text makes their learning a more concrete goal to attain vs reading and being asked to "take notes," which is a very tough ask, full of assumptions about just what that entails.

Templates are fairly simple to scaffold, and unlike generic graphic organizers, your templates can include prompts very specific to your audience and their knowledge. Include word banks and starter images or partially fill out a template leaving space for particular words/phrases or supporting imagery. Include sentence frames with language non-negotiables. For many learners, multi-step directions plus new information plus translating plus miscellaneous distractors can quickly overwhelm. Housing all of this in one place helps them navigate at their own pace.

They are simple (albeit not always "easier") formative assessments. I can easily circulate through the class to see where the sticking points are and make adjustments on the fly. Gaps are readily apparent which can help students self-assess and make their own learning plan for where they need to focus their efforts next.

Since the templates I use might cover more than one lesson or meeting, I've learned it's easier to keep track of them than it is multiple pieces of paper. I've also noticed more pride in the presentation of the extended notes with many of my students or participants taking them home to color-code them or re-write them, even at the high school level.

Creating templates also refines the lesson or presentation planning process as presenters reflect on what they really want participants to walk away knowing that day, that week, or in that unit.

Cons: If you have a creative audience, templates will limit them, so I provide choice. Those who I know can rock the task without a template get to do what they do best, as long as they include the necessary information in some way.

Speaking of limits, if users believe the template is all they need, they may rely on superficial information to fill in the spaces. Push them, continue to question them as they write and sketch.

Some view visual note templates as the end-all be-all of learning. They are not. They are meant to be used as a supportive stepping stone to something further such as a Socratic seminar, writing activity, compare/contrast an improved oral presentation, question development, discussion boost, or a shared reference from a meeting.

See Appendix B for more examples.

PLANNING

GOALS

students | teacher | audience

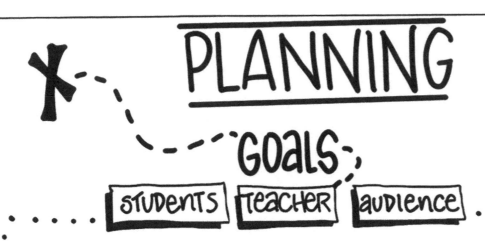

CRITICAL TALKING POINTS

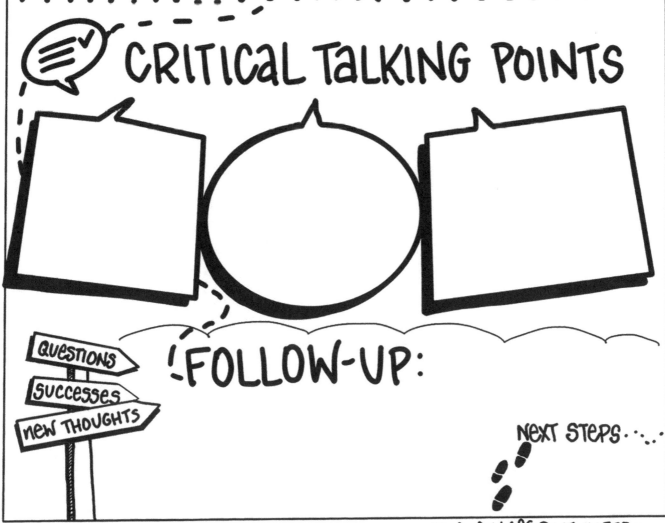

FOLLOW-UP:

QUESTIONS
SUCCESSES
NEW THOUGHTS

NEXT STEPS

• WENDI PILLARS @WENDI322 •

HOOK:
(INTRO)

QUICK ACTIVITY to BUILD or ACTIVATE STUDENTS' BACKGROUND KNOWLEDGE

DATE: _____
CLASS: _____

MATERIALS NEEDED:

DIRECT INSTRUCTION:

CLEAR OBJECTIVES; STUDENTS READ, WRITE & SPEAK USING CONTENT LANGUAGE

OPPORTUNITIES for:
- ☐ LISTENING ____
- ☐ SPEAKING ____
- ☐ READING ____
- ☐ WRITING ____

STUDENT PRACTICE:

TEACHER MODELS & EXPLAINS EXPECTATIONS & PROCEDURES; ACTIVELY ENGAGED IN READING, WRITING, SPEAKING ABOUT TOPIC.

VOCAB:

REFER to WORDS OFTEN; CONSISTENTLY USE in CONTEXT ORALLY & IN WRITING

WENDI PILLARS @ WENDI322

ASSESSMENT:

MONITOR PROGRESS, PROVIDE FEEDBACK; DEMONSTRATE NEW LEARNING ORALLY or IN WRITING

NOTES:

SUPPORTS: — GRAPHIC ORGANIZERS — MULTIMEDIA — SENTENCE FRAME — VISUALS — WORD BANKS — FLEXIBLE GROUPING

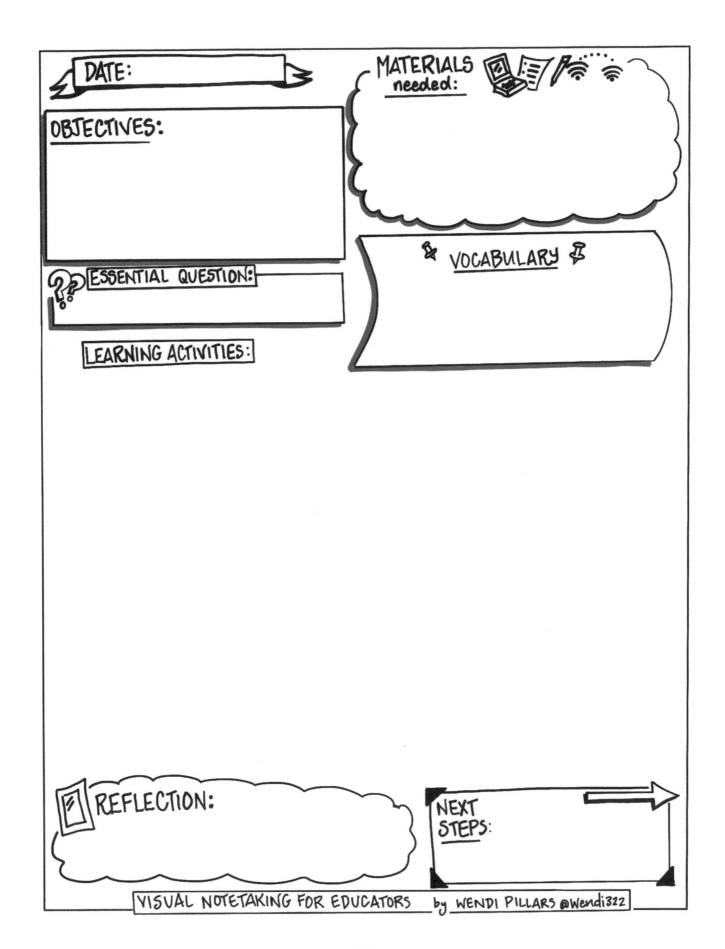

DATE:

OBJECTIVES:

MATERIALS needed:

VOCABULARY

?? ESSENTIAL QUESTION:

LEARNING ACTIVITIES:

REFLECTION:

NEXT STEPS:

VISUAL NOTETAKING FOR EDUCATORS   by WENDI PILLARS @Wendi322

Time

We affectionately call them "helium hands," those participants in our meetings or classes whose hands raise before we even get the question out of our mouths. Often, they might skip the hand raise and just blurt out the answer. Great to keep things moving along. Not so great for most of our audience members, however, and here's why.

Did you know the typical wait time presenters use after posing a question is less than a second?

Less than a second! To process what was just asked. Think about a question. Interpret it even if it's not in your home language. Process an answer. Translate that response into English. Take a breath for confidence. Raise hand. Only to realize the speaker is on to the next question. Oof.

The time to sketch, to really see or understand the content, is time for introverts, struggling learners, language learners, and others to be successful rather than be left out when the more confident learners, extroverts, and speedy thinkers synthesize and respond much more quickly. Wait time is a Big Deal and sketching allows needed processing to happen sans awkwardness.

That being said, a huge pushback I hear from colleagues is that "there's not enough time" to sketch when you "have to get through ALL. That. Content." I completely understand that pressure, so my question to my colleagues and to my readers stems from my own experiences: what's the use of rushing through content if your audience isn't retaining any of it? I'd far rather have them remember a percentage of it well instead of nothing at all.

When judging the value of taking time in a meeting or class to sketch, here are two guidelines I follow remembering how they support wait time:

1. Chunk your lesson or presentation: pre-plan stopping points along with timed intervals between them. You're probably already doing this! Quick sketches can align with brain breaks every fifteen to twenty minutes or so, honing in on and consolidating specific parts of the content that lend themselves to visuals, your objectives, more intriguing or accessible ideas, vocabulary, or particular sequences.

2. Limit sketch time: one to three minutes is sufficient for a quick formative assessment, for time to think through a response with detail, and critically, for each individual student to show what they understand. Maximize this time by circulating around the room, asking helpful questions and pushing for more detail if necessary. Misconceptions can be addressed on the spot and opportunities for sharing out can be provided. Letting it drag out too long can be counterproductive, although be flexible if you still see that people are actually working.

Practice embracing silence after asking a question with visual notes, even in the margin or on a sticky note. Extending wait time allows others to formulate their thinking into more critical and nuanced responses. If you're aiming for a larger page-size visual note, chunking time and information will certainly aid the overall process. If you want a visual note to be created over the course of days, that's perfectly fine and has its own myriad benefits of revisiting, revising, and deepening connections. Just get started and enjoy learning more about others' thinking.

Tips for Visual Notetakers

Here is a one-pager with tips for using visual notes in your classroom. These can also be translated for use in the boardroom (substitute "student" for team member, leaders, visual thinker). If you remember nothing but these tips, you'll be alright.

Of course, you know me by now, but I want you to think of how you could use this format in your meetings, your classroom, or your organization. What are the top tips you want to communicate to others about your content, your product, or your process? What are top tips for studying or being successful in your class, according to students? What are top tips for being the best version of yourself at school, at work, and at home? Is there a simple color palette that supports your thinking?

Consider the format of the visual note: How can you or your organization take a more complex concept and whittle it down into six tips or steps? What thinking processes occur when you try to simplify something complex for others to understand?

Have team members or students choose a business or academic challenge, hobby, or favorite activity and create a tip sheet similar to this. Share. Inform. Educate. Entertain . . . Choice and voice *and* getting to know your co-workers, teammates, and students? Yes, please.

Visual Notetaking
TIPS FOR CLASSROOM SUCCESS — WENDI PILLARS @WENDI322

1 ASK STUDENTS: "HOW CAN WE REPRESENT THIS (CONCEPT/IDEA/TEXT, etc.) WITH A VISUAL?"

★ Great Brain Break   ★ INDIVIDUAL OR w/ PARTNER   ★ excellent Formative assessment

2 NEVER JUDGE A STUDENT'S ART ABILITIES. FOCUS ON THE PROCESS, MEANING, & CONNECTIONS!

PROCESS / ❀pretty❀

3 FOCUS ON A DARKER BASE COLOR WITH ONE OR TWO HIGHLIGHT COLORS

◯◯◯ + ◯◯◯, etc.

4 MODEL EXPECTATIONS & NAVIGATE IDEAS TOGETHER.

GIVE STUDENTS THE MARKER!

IT'S OK! (PROMISE!)

5 THE WORSE YOU DRAW, THE MORE INVITING IT IS FOR STUDENTS TO TRY.

MISS, I CAN DO BETTER THAN THAT!   WHAT IS THAT?

★ MODELS GROWTH MINDSET   ★ MAKES IT FUN

6 USE THE VISUALS AS A REFERENCE. THEY ARE STILL NOTES!

DISPLAY

- ADD MORE DETAILS
- HIGHLIGHT KEY IDEAS/TERMS
- COMPARE/CONTRAST W/PEERS
- SHARE DIGITALLY FOR FEEDBACK

Tools of My Trade

In class, I keep my tools simple:

Document camera, copy paper, notepaper, or recycled paper with a Flair pen for visibility are my most used tools. Because I always share classrooms, using the whiteboard isn't the most practical, but it's my second most-used canvas for visual notes, or for my students to join in. Every once in a while, I will use my iPad with screen mirroring in class, but I'm intentional about it. I don't feel it's completely fair for me to have access to that technology when my students don't.

(*With remote learning, I do use my iPad increasingly more as a whiteboard so that we can take notes together or I can explain concepts as needed for clarity. I also rely on a flipchart for remote teaching because I feel its "human touch" is valuable for those on marathon virtual meeting days to have some semblance of a screen break.)

Students use pens, sometimes pencils (although I encourage them to use non-erasable writing utensils so they can own their mistakes), colored pencils, and sometimes Crayola markers or refillable whiteboard markers. Sometimes I make sketchbooks for them by folding copy paper in two and adding a colorful cover because it's easier to keep track of.

When I work professionally, I do use my iPad to create sketches, and I also rely on my iPad to create templates or time-lapse videos for class. My markers of choice for analog work are Neuland markers because I like the color palettes and the fact that they're refillable. They also don't bleed through paper, and the colors don't fade like other markers do. I don't let my students use them because they are more expensive, but I will use them to create anchor charts for class that I hope to use for a while since the colors remain vibrant without fading.

In workshops, I again rely on flipcharts and markers, and my iPad and computer for projecting images created ahead of time and in the moment for explanation and modeling.

TOOLS of my TRADE

CLASSROOM MARKERS
- crayola -

- in class
- group & individual use
- durable
- economical

iPad

apple pencil

- creating templates
- time-lapse videos
- notes at home
- occasional use in class

- notebook paper
- copy paper
- flair pen
- pen

- whiteboard
- chart paper
- whiteboard markers

- document camera

WENDI PILLARS @ WENDI322

Universality of Icons & Symbols

You may have heard of famous cave paintings in the Caves of Lascaux France, nicknamed the prehistoric Sistine Chapel, or the stunning colored paintings of the Altamira Caves in Spain that date back over 35,000 years. Artistic expression has always been a part of humanity, including both line drawings and abstract imagery.

When teaching others about visual thinking, share information about the universality and enduring influence of pictures, paintings, and artistic renderings that have been uncovered over the years. Humans have relied on imagery for thousands of years, so why shouldn't we rely more on visual thinking? Even the enigmatic "unknown" imagery provokes wonder, while clearer picture messages honor stories of long ago. Pictures that are *universally* known.

Renowned paleoarchaeologist Genevieve von Petzinger has been researching geometric images in cave paintings. She has discovered and catalogued thirty-two symbols from fifty-two caves across continents.[13] Their consistency suggests they weren't haphazard lines, and it's fascinating to know they were found on every current continent except Antarctica, in an age without real-time communication or travel opportunities. What a great—and a bit controversial—topic for statistics, graphing, geography, history, and definitions of language.

Another example is the American Hobo[14] subculture in the era of the Great Depression and its development of signs and symbols to communicate with each other. While many were illiterate, American Hobos developed a visual system of signs and symbols unfamiliar to outsiders to communicate a range of potentially life-saving information. Water towers, curbs, and fenceposts were just some of their canvases, carved with instructive symbols revealing someone who could provide water and bread, whether a house had vicious dogs, or whether they could sleep in a barn, for example. How would that work today, 100 years later?

The famed Rijksmuseum of Amsterdam initiated a #StartDrawing[15] campaign to encourage visitors to sketch what they loved rather than move through the museum snapping endless selfies without actually *looking* and appreciating the details of the art. Visitors can grab sketch paper and a pencil and are encouraged not to worry about making beautiful art themselves, but rather to see things they've never noticed before. We can all learn from that advice.

Rethink common communication symbols that inform our days. From our phone apps to bathroom signs, from computer icons to cow and camel branding symbols, students and organizational team members can collect fascinating examples from their environment. Especially tap into your audience's varied cultural experiences and ask them to weigh in on signs that are new for them, or signs they used to see in their home countries.

What universal signs do you know and would help you if you traveled somewhere foreign?

universality

◇ Be ready to defend yourself

▭• DANGEROUS NEIGHBORHOOD

◯◯ DON'T GIVE UP

DOCTOR NO CHARGE

UNSAFE PLACE

COPS INACTIVE

8 △△△ KIND WOMAN

SAMPLING of AMERICAN HOBO SIGNS & SYMBOLS

Innate desire to honor stories with pictures.

V∧ OPEN ANGLE

1 CLAVIFORM

CROSSHATCH

Ɇ PECTIFORM

✳ ASTERISK

◯ CIRCLE

Ƨ ZIGZAG

@ SPIRAL

Y Y-SIGN

⋮ DOTS

↑ TECTIFORM

Ψ PENNIFORM

cave symbols

⋆ GEOMETRIC SYMBOLS OUTNUMBERED DRAWINGS of PEOPLE & animals
  • creativity, imagination, abstract thought

⋆ 32 SIGNS WORLDWIDE
  • repetition with little variation
  • stylized representations
  • not an alphabet

Virtual Visuals,
Part 1: The Relevance of Hand Drawing

As this book goes to print, much of the world is learning how to conquer Zoom fatigue or simple computer screen exhaustion, thanks to COVID-19. As a presenter, speaker, or educator, remember that hand-drawn visuals are still relevant for boosting interest and inspiration.

Despite seeing others on a tiny screen (if at all), I challenge you to think of how you can incorporate hand-drawn images of different sizes. Doing so will activate people's attention, support, and enhance understanding, memory retention, and their engagement levels. Simply asking participants to display their notes on camera is a robust tactic for individual accountability and sharing one's learning. That's a huge win in my estimation.

Quick tips to start: 1) Incorporate hand-drawn pictures into your PowerPoint or on index cards to hold up to the screen during your meeting or class. 2) Set up a flipchart next to you so you can elicit ideas from the group online and they can see you drawing and writing. 3) Use the flipchart with a template that you fill in together as a group, or 4) use it for transitions with instructions or as a tool for providing a big picture overview. Let your imagination fly! You'll realize analog is still cool, with its inherent humanity and flexibility. Your audience can see you, they can see your hands and your work with different markers, and they can think and anticipate right alongside you. Worried about perfection? Some insist that our brains work a bit harder when viewing imperfect drawings, so think of imperfection as a bonus! We should absolutely draw even if—especially if—we don't understand something. However rudimentary our sketches, they have the power to better help us describe, discuss, and understand even the most complex issues.

Share work easily: 1) Encourage virtual meeting participants to always have something to write with and write on so they can create quick sketches off-screen, awaken fine motor movement, provoke creativity, and provide time to still the mind, even if only for a few minutes. 2) Have participants show their drawings on camera simultaneously or individually, or share their work in smaller breakout groups. 3) Invite more voices by spotlighting some and asking them to explain their sketch or their thinking behind it. 4) Encourage comments verbally or in the chat box, leveraging these extra options from what we have available in person.

Another alternative is for you to upload hand-drawn sketches into your presentation for a welcomed variation from static or overused stock imagery. Hand-drawn sketches created either digitally or with markers serve as a powerful shift from predictably soporific PowerPoint slides.

With technology, it's critical to remember that learning comes first, with fancy features and functions coming after. Don't let the overwhelm of choice deter you from your ultimate goals of communication and understanding. Your greatest test will be your audience, so provide some space to let markers do their magic, and be open to ideas that serve as exciting points of departure.

*For a list of some common current platforms used to collaborate visually, see the Appendix, but please keep in mind that these can be fluid and vary in accessibility.

Visual Library

This is your holy grail. One of your first tasks is to create a visual collection, a visual library, if you will, of common subjects, verbs, icons, symbols—you name it—that appear throughout your curriculum or business. The more you collect, the quicker you'll be able to access your "vocabulary," which then makes communication more efficient.

Comb through your objectives, goals, vision statement, standards, common topics, ideas that are continually recycled or spiraled throughout the course, polysemous (multiple meaning) words that can be easily confused, sticking points for your learners or customers based on past experiences, and ideas that are just plain fun to visualize. Once you start considering your content through a visual lens, you'll find more items to sketch. As it becomes more routine you can start banking images created to use as models for others.

Think, too, about processes and routines you have in your classroom and organization. Events of the day? The writing process? How to podcast, how to jigsaw an article, presentation tips . . . what are the *processes* that you need to scaffold for your learners until they internalize it? Anchor charts with brief text and simple visual steps can make your life easier. How can you make routines more dynamic with visuals? And about those PowerPoints . . . what if you added just a couple of hand-drawn sketches to break up your slides? If you're just not sure what sketch to create, again, ask students or teammates to help you build the charts and tell you what is helpful. Boom. There's your buy-in, more nuanced understanding, and willingness to pay attention.

If you are wondering how the heck to get started with "what to draw," the next page has some ideas I plucked directly from the social sciences standards. I literally went through the standards, pulled out key words and ideas, listed them, then started sketching. I stopped after one page! Even a single page demonstrates how rich our content is for visual imagery and I am nowhere near an expert in this subject area. I would love to live in content area expert brains for a hot minute so I could mine the treasures you hold! Draw that awesome-ness out!

Another consideration is your imagery organization, whether digital or analog. Bear in mind that a single element could represent multiple ideas, so be flexible and open to multiple creative interpretations. This means they fit in more than one category, so file them in more than one place if you need to. If you're not feeling super confident as you practice drawing a new visual, know that simple word labels can go a long way in helping contextualize what you draw.

Finally, think about more ways and places to use your visual vocabulary. Sprinkle them in your Power-Points and keynotes, use them in meetings, in the classroom, in minutes or newsletters . . . the choices are endless. The more frequently you use them, the more automatic your retrieval will become; this automaticity frees up thinking to focus more on capturing content.

What else can you think of?

*More starter pages for your visual library can be found in the Appendices.

SOCIAL SCIENCES

ROYALTY

DOCUMENT / AGREEMENT

WRITING

INQUIRY / INVESTIGATION

SLAVERY

BATTLEFIELD / WAR / BATTLE / FIGHT / MILITARY

GLOBE / PLANET EARTH

MAP / JOURNEY DESTINATION / LOCATION

NATIONALISM / AMERICA / COUNTRY

VOTE

DIVERSITY / INCLUSION

SOCIAL JUSTICE VOICE / PEACE

WENDI PILLARS @Wendi322

Vision Statement

Think about your vision and/or mission statement. Can you recite it off the top of your head? More importantly, can your team members do the same?

I'm not sure about you, but all of the organizations I've worked in have had statements full of jargon, edu-speak, corporate-speak, or whatever you want to call it.

I've never memorized a single one.

Maybe I should but it's always a lot of "noise," words without substance. Maybe they sound great as we check the required boxes for "posting our mission and vision" on expensive banners near the front door. But if you really want people to FOLLOW and BE INSPIRED BY your organization's mission and vision, wouldn't it make sense to ensure anyone can remember it?

How can you make your statements more memorable, more dynamic? How can you make them something your team can internalize? How can you simplify it down to the absolute essence? Who should know it and why? Should students and staff at a school know it, follow it, believe it? Only staff? Why or why not? Should customers know it? Or community members? If they knew it, would it make a difference?

Use the template to think through key ideas and compare with a colleague, your Personal Learning Community (PLC), and leadership teams. As always, what you think are key ideas may not the same as what others think. Compare, revise, revamp. All in the name of inspiring and unifying organizational purpose.

VISION/MISSION STATEMENT:

REACTION of STAFF/STUDENTS:

CURRENT

VS.

IDEAL

WHAT NEEDS to CHANGE?

WHAT DOESN'T?

OK

"REAL" GOALS:
(What do you REALLY want your statement to say?)

EXPLAIN YOUR VISION to a TODDLER:

HOW CAN YOU REPRESENT THAT WITH A VISUAL?

KEY WORDS/ CONCEPTS:

NEW and IMPROVED STATEMENT:

Visual Representation

Using the ideas from the template on the previous page, now consider the top ten icons that represent your ideas. They don't have to be perfect, and you can certainly change them later, but actually sketching them now will help crystallize your thinking.

Hold a graphic jam with colleagues, staff, coaches, leaders, customers, or PLC teammates. Have each person sketch what they believe are the top ten visuals that represent the key ideas of your organization as it is or as you envision it to be. Set a time limit so that it's clear these are not expected to be perfect sketches.

Ask yourselves the following questions:

- What is it that you talk about the most?
- What do you focus on, or, perhaps, where do you want to divert thinking?
- What do you envision?
- What does success look like?
- What are common misconceptions that need to be addressed?
- How can you represent these ideas visually in your statement?
- And, hey, above all else, does your vision have "vision?"

I've included some common icons found in business and education that you can trace or copy to get started, but I encourage uniqueness and veering away from the cliche.

What else can you add to make it yours?

Our new vision:

Our plan to REACH, SUPPORT & GROW all STUDENTS & STAFF members.

Visual Notetaking Template

This template was designed for colleagues a few years ago, with pertinent considerations all on one page, and has been in continual demand so I wanted to share it with you. Beginning from the top where it says, "Visual Notes according to ___," let's take a clockwise tour.

Go-to content icons/ symbols: Choose ten visual images that represent words and/or concepts you refer to the most often in your context. Practice sketching them in a way that is recognizable, quick, and simple to draw. Ask others for ideas if you're stuck, and use the representations as a shared reference or a type of shorthand.

Other planning considerations to ask yourself:

- Chunking: what amount of sketching will my audience create and what type of information am I looking for?

- Objectives: what are the learning objectives? Are they clear and are my visual note tasks/ expectations aligned with them? How will visual notes help learners reach those goals?

- Possible uses: be explicit with participants how their notes will be used. Will they be a personal study tool? Brainstorming tool to be revised over time? Shared with a partner? On display for a larger audience? Used as part of a presentation in front of a group? Will there be an opportunity to justify and explain parts of the visual if desired or needed?

- Time: how long will the participants have to create their sketches? One to two-minute brain breaks or information recaps? Three to five minutes to compare and contrast sketches with others? Longer time for more details? And what will the interval time be—one sketch every fifteen minutes of the meeting or class? Weekly? Five times per unit? Be specific.

Go-to sketch apps: I keep life pretty simple. Most of my work revolves around these apps listed. Students have limited access, so we create a LOT with just pen and paper.

Questions to ask: Plan questions ahead of time, but these two questions are non-negotiable: "How can we represent that with a visual?" and "Tell me about your sketch." No judgments.

Determine layout: You can find more about this in the organization section, but consider whether a particular layout would be better for meeting objectives, OR if you just make space for learners to let their own layout emerge, driven by the information they receive. Often, organic layouts are as telling as the sketch content itself about what someone is learning and hearing.

Key words: Please tell me you have specific words you want to represent and include visually!

Make connections: Encourage visual thinkers to find and highlight connections between facts and ideas, opinions, people, actions, and more, using arrows, lines, and whatever their imaginations devise.

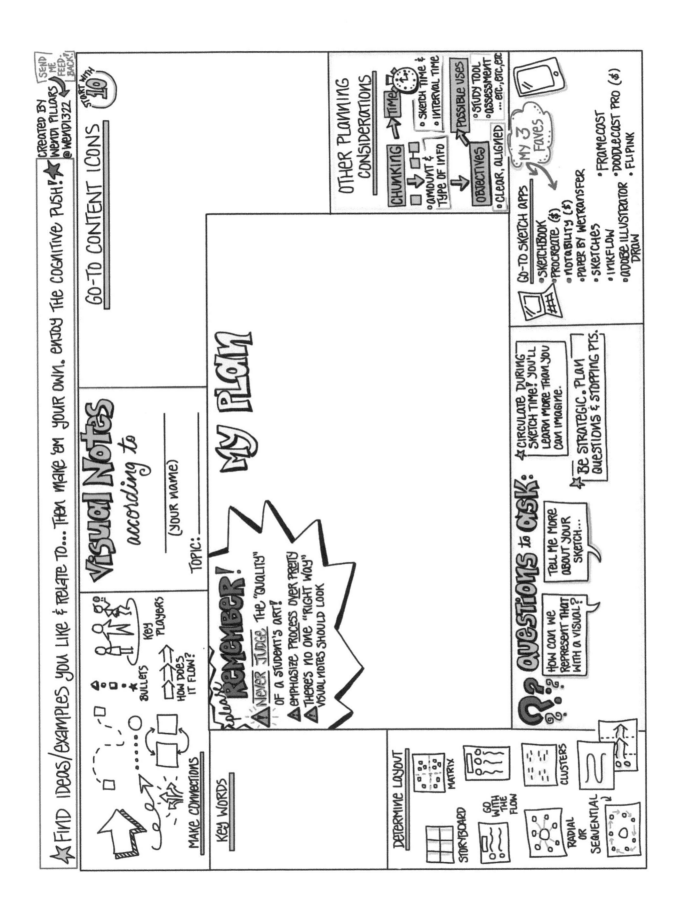

Warm-Ups,
Part 1: Imagination & Innovation

Use your imagination for warm-ups. These are fun ways to introduce sketching to students and audiences at the start of presentations or class, but I have also found them useful for transitions into a new topic, brain breaks, or even to calm learners if they need some space or time, no matter the reason. Yep, warm-ups "draw" them in. (See what I did there?)

Doing these types of activities encourages laughter and a way of experiencing flow. There is possibility, freedom, and heck, everything might just be one big mistake, but you learn not to hesitate as much, and you learn that it all ends up okay in the end. Bonus, you and your group, team, or learners have pushed what you can do just a little bit further, may have found a design, style, or new pen that speaks to them, and may have gained at least a smidge of confidence in their lines.

Some examples on the next page include writing or drawing your name or a simple sketch upside down and using your non-dominant hand. Draw a house with the roof on the ground and the door in the sky, print or handwrite your name upside down. It doesn't take a lot to wake up your brain and think about things from an entirely new point of view. Draw with music, draw standing up for that bigger whole-body range of motion in front of large paper or a whiteboard, draw with eyes closed, one continuous line or a combination of the above.

Bottom line benefits or warm-ups? No judgment, a lot of fun, and a license to be different. Just drawing simple lines and circles will entice personalities and patterns to emerge, kids and adults alike. (It's interesting to watch the initial hesitancy even in warm-ups, because we're so used to wanting to do things "the right way.") Use this time to play. Pinky promise that your visual thinkers will learn about themselves and your community will gain a whole new vibe. Warm-ups are also a time to hone fine motor skills while preparing more awakened brains for learning and innovative participation.

WARM-UP

GET THOSE THINKING "MUSCLES" READY!

- **DRAW UPSIDE DOWN***

- **USE NON-DOMINANT HAND**

How do I even HOLD this pen?!

HOUSE

* ADVANCED MODEL DEMONSTRATED

* FOR US MERE MORTALS TURN THE PAPER UPSIDE DOWN

SIZE it UP!

POSSIBILITIES!

- **DRAW WITH ♪ MUSIC**

- **DRAW STANDING UP!**
  - BIGGER RANGE of MOTION
  - WHOLE BODY MOVEMENT

- **ONE CONTINUOUS LINE**

  JUST MOVE YOUR PAPER WITHOUT LIFTING the MARKER

→ WITH MUSIC
→ BIGGER PAPER
→ NON-DOMINANT HAND

- **EYES CLOSED**

WENDI PILLARS @WENDI322

Warm-Ups,
Part 2: Permission to Play

Pretty simple ideas, but sparks are important so you can gather traction for your own ideas. Play with lines, shapes, and tools.

YOU HAVE PERMISSION TO PLAY.

Warm-ups add fun and are an opportunity for slightly guided creativity (in case there are those with blank page fears), muscle memory development, and fine motor skill development. All of which are simple ways to build confidence. If your visual thinkers are daunted by large white spaces, I recommend starting with small boxes or spaces. They're less daunting and they are perfect for timed breaks if you only want to take a couple of minutes during transitions, as participants or students come into the room, etc.

Shapes can be guided to somehow relate to the current content. Or not. For this, I actually recommend letting kids and adults alike to do their own thing to explore and experiment. Providing opportunities also provides choice which also helps promote confidence for thinking visually, one chunk at a time.

This kind of work can be pretty meditative, so be mindful of your timing—might it be useful at the beginning of class on Monday mornings as students come into the room and transition from being at home on the weekend? Or mid-day break when there are marathon meetings at work? How about a mid-week breather? Or a Friday afternoon time to recap the week in a unique way? What if you simply added a rectangle or other basic shape like these here on tests and meeting handouts to remind your teams or learners to be creative, if only in a smaller space?

One design leads to another

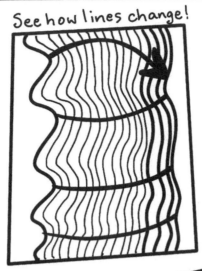

See how lines change!

Simple practice

Shape distortion

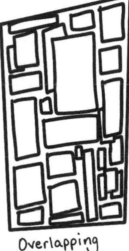

Overlapping

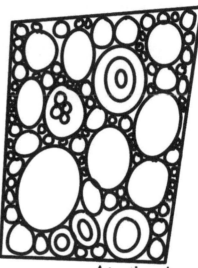

Adapting shape to space available

PLAY WITH SHAPES & LINES

- Permission to play
- Practice shape distortion
- Fine motor skill development
- Small boxes are less daunting → success in chunks
- Muscle memory
- Get comfortable with your tools

WENDI PILLARS @ WENDI322

What's happening (mentally) as you take visual notes?

I still get asked if I'm going to "draw pictures" in class or at conferences, and this highlights for me what is happening in the brain when we take visual notes. Whether during listening or reading, or a combination of inputs, there is a constant flow of decision-making, unparalleled by any other form of notetaking I've encountered.

It's a delightfully intense cognitive push.

Revisit the purpose for notetaking, including who the intended audience will be, then distinguish between process and product, especially if any type of assessment or follow-up is at play. Teach learners about what their brains are doing, because it helps develop their mindset in productive ways. Doing so helps address "overwhelm" with new understanding about why they're feeling that way, and they can celebrate the layers of success that come with visible measures of growth in notetaking abilities. My learners and workshop participants have said it "hurts their brain" to create visual notes, to revise, revisit, make connections, and subsequently apply the knowledge they've gained. I take that as a good sign

What other style of notetaking entails so much mental activity in your classes or in meetings? Add in collaborative efforts with conversations, comparisons, debates, and subsequent decision-making and you've just raised the cognitive bar even higher. As leaders, isn't this what we want for our meeting attendees and learners?

WHAT'S HAPPENING
as you and your students TAKE VISUAL NOTES?

When you assess consider whether you are looking at **process** or **product** because there's a <u>LOT</u> happening in the brain at once!

It's no Wonder my students say their brain hurts when they create visual notes!

WHAT DO I ALREADY KNOW?

SAVE INFORMATION for LATER?

DOES THIS INFO "FIT" BETTER ELSEWHERE?

MAIN IDEAS vs. DETAILS

TYPOGRAPHY & FONT: STYLE, SIZE, TONE

DECISIONMAKING

BORDERS, CONTAINERS & CONNECTORS to HELP ORGANIZE

PLACEMENT on the PAGE

CENTRAL FOCUS or ANCHORING PHENOMENON

WHAT INFORMATION to INCLUDE or EXCLUDE

LANDSCAPE or PORTRAIT ORIENTATION

WHO WILL SEE THIS?

WHO IS MY AUDIENCE?

AMPLIFY or MINIMIZE DETAILS?

WHAT is the PURPOSE for THESE NOTES?

IS THERE ROOM for NEW INFORMATION or QUESTIONS?

WHAT DO I NEED to INCLUDE SO THAT IT MAKES SENSE for THEM?

WHICH COLORS SHOULD I USE?

ADD MORE LABELS? MORE PICTURES?

PERSONAL IDEAS & HUMOR INCLUDED or SERIOUS FACTS ONLY?

PRE-DETERMINED ORGANIZATION or EMERGENT FORMAT/ FREEHAND

BUT, MY DRAWINGS!

HOW CAN I REPRESENT THIS IDEA BETTER

DID I LISTEN WELL ENOUGH to HONOR the SPEAKER?

... ETC., ...

WENDI PILLARS @ WENDI322

Writing,
Part 1: Images as Support

I'm willing to bet that most of you have used imagery in some fashion for writing with your students, maybe as part of prewriting or brainstorming, or maybe as illustrations to bring writing to life. So, this isn't new. When you bring words and pictures together, a little bit of magic happens. Ideas tend to flow more readily when you have a picture or image in your head since you can already delve deeper into the details before you start writing. There's actually a word for that: "transmediation," when meaning from one system (pictures) is recast to another (writing). Pretty sweet, especially when it supports students who have little affinity for words, let alone wordsmithing.

How can visual notes help your learners with writing beyond prewriting, brainstorming, or illustrating? Instead of having them write an introduction about themselves at the beginning of the semester, have them create a sketch of themselves that includes their goals, likes, dislikes, dreams, or whatever might pertain to your context. It's definitely more fun to share and captures the attention of peers in a memorable way. Asking visual thinkers to picture themselves in positions of success, AND others' reactions to them, triggers the visualization effect that athletes and others rely upon. Research has shown that visualizing your goals is powerful, but writing them down with an image is exponentially so. Imagine adding a higher likelihood of success just from taking the time and cognitive prowess to sketch oneself in that position!

Sharing or displaying sketches, even for short amounts of time, can initiate more organic conversations among your learners while providing some movement to get the blood flowing. They can see others' interpretations of the same topic, see what they may have missed, and what they agree or disagree with. They can also consider the style of the visuals, to see what elements they like most. As the facilitator, pose questions in writing that are related to the sketches: what do you notice? What would you add? What other connections can you find and see?, etc. Choose to focus on one or two elements at a time and build from there.

> " Everybody walks past a thousand story ideas everyday. The good writers are the ones who see five or six of them. Most people don't see any. "
> — Orson Scott

writing:

INSTEAD OF PARAGRAPH-FORMAT AUTOBIOGRAPHIES OR GOAL-SETTING IN PURE TEXT, STUDENTS CAN SKETCH THEIR IDEAL SELVES THEN LABEL.

goals · dislikes · context · likes · big ideas · anticipated obstacles · background details · clothing details · reactions of others to your success

ETC...

THEN PRESENT SKETCHES VIA A GALLERY WALK.

★ STUDENTS CAN:
- compare/contrast
- complete "I wonder... I see..." and other written prompts
- make myriad connections
- provide constructive written feedback in digital or analog form

★ OTHERS' REPRESENTATIONS HELP **SPARK** IDEAS!

USE SKETCHES TO PROMPT AS MANY connections AS POSSIBLE, BOTH INTERNAL & EXTERNAL.

TRY LARGER PAPER to encourage larger motor movement & to build confidence!

WENDI PILLARS @Wendi322

Writing,
Part 2: Easy Integrations

With my newest language learners, we often begin class with a writing warm-up together. I include picture clues with the sentences to provide some anticipatory background for the day's objectives, or I write something about the students themselves using new vocabulary and a bit of exaggeration. For practice and for fun, I might also write sentences about the students with everyday vocabulary: Luis is wearing a striped shirt. Katarin has a new bracelet on her wrist.

Asking students to sketch a favorite part of the story, a favorite character, a prediction for the next chapter, or develop a scene using three vocabulary words, for example, can all stimulate the visual thinking muscles. When they share their work, it helps with their oral fluency, and if they can say it, chances are good they can then write it more easily. Sketching sparks their thinking; it's often so difficult to start writing cold; modeling for students that they can draw rough sketches and return to them as they write convinces learners that the goal is not perfection. Revising work can also include revising sketches!

Another way to incorporate sketches is to build them into feedback and thank-you letters to classroom guests. Students can sketch the guest expert (be it a Cherokee Indian, shark scientist, or immigration activist—who knows!) doing their work, complete with tools, thinking bubbles, and stating facts and words of wisdom for others. It doubles as feedback so you can see what they've learned from the guest speaker and it keeps learners more eager to remain focused. The visuals can be shared with the guests soon after and they love this type of feedback. They can literally see at a glance what resonated most with students!

writing:

- **LABEL** SKETCHES WITH SINGLE WORDS, PHRASES or SENTENCES

- USE VISUALS to **CLARIFY** & JUMP-START WRITING

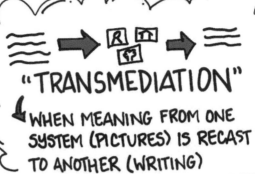

"TRANSMEDIATION"

WHEN MEANING FROM ONE SYSTEM (PICTURES) IS RECAST TO ANOTHER (WRITING)

 VISUALIZING ADDRESSES **WAIT TIME** → EQUITY in "RESPONSE-ABILITY"

AUTHENTIC AUDIENCE

 TRY A *peer preview*

STUDENTS USE SKETCHES to TALK THROUGH THEIR STORIES & WRITING PLANS

 **STOP...** and **SYNTHESIZE**
"Sassy point"

- PRE-DETERMINED STOPPING POINTS in LESSON; SKETCH & 2-3 SYNTHESIZING SENTENCES

- STEPPING STONES for MORE DETAILED RESPONSES

 TRY *thank-you* NOTES

 SKETCH TAKEAWAYS from GUEST SPEAKERS, AUTHORS, VOLUNTEERS

* SERVES as FEEDBACK, too!

ADD VISUALS to SHARED WRITING

WENDI PILLARS @Wendi322

Xenoglossy

Haha! You were wondering what I might have up my proverbial sleeve for X! This couldn't be more perfect because YOU have xenoglossy! And YOU have xenoglossy! she says in her best Oprah voice.

Simply put, xenoglossy is the ability to speak a language without having "formally" learned it, and you, my friends, can speak visual despite never having had formal training. Using visuals to make ourselves more effectively understood, more memorable, or to make ideas more shareable has helped make our world an easier place to live for thousands of years.

Developing your visual language is akin to learning a new language because you're learning how to communicate, think, and process in new ways with imagery instead of linguistic words. When you're thinking about how to get started or how to organize your visual vocabulary, think of what you already know. Then think about topics you might encounter next. If you're in the classroom, choose go-to content icons or school-based imagery. Whether you're in an environmental, sports, political, or medical organizations (to name a few), develop an imagery bank aligned with your particular area and how you want others to view you.

Ever had to repeat instructions for a task in your workshop, meeting, or classroom? (Asking for a friend.) It might interest you to know that people "following directions with text and illustrations do 323% better than people following directions without illustrations."[16] 323%?! Wow. As a teacher and speaker, I believe in that difference, and I definitely want to make sure I use that support!

Did you know that tweets with images receive 150% more retweets than those without, that snapchat users upload 9000 photos per minute, and that there are more than 500 million active Instagram users every day.[17, 18] It doesn't take much to "see" how social media is revolutionizing communication. Knowing that our brains process images exponentially faster than text sure makes it seem silly NOT to include them when we want to make our information more memorable and understandable. Illustrated text is nine percent more effective than text alone when testing immediate comprehension and eighty-three percent more effective when the test was delayed.[19] Appropriate visuals can reduce explanation time and increase learner confidence as they begin to organize ideas, find patterns and relationships, and ultimately, comprehend more when they read and listen. Which then leads to higher achievement.

Visuals—they're unequivocally a global language so it would behoove us as educators and organizational leaders to become more intentional about literacy in the visual language people use every day. Visual literacy is the secret sauce of learning, which then leads to action. We have the seeds of it. Let's make growth imminent.

Yes to YOU

Have you ever been plagued by doubt about your ability to do something? Or maybe not just to do something but to do it well? Well enough that others won't laugh at you? Or disrespect your process or outcome?

This page is for you. And maybe for your team members and fellow learners. Seriously, dear readers, I struggle and worry about being able to provide what I need for my learners, listeners, and readers every single day and it would take a lifetime to get over that anxiety. When I sketch in meetings, workshops, or classrooms, though, even for five minutes, I'm reminded that I can help participants capture their learning with time to express what they know in often unique ways. I sketch right along with them, sometimes letting them see what I'm doing if I feel that support is important. Other times I might wait until everyone is done to reveal my ideas because I want them to know that their ideas are more important to me.

Sketching in real-time keeps me present and keeps me in tune with what my learners understand. I have only recently (in the past few years) understood Just How Much I Rely on Creating Visuals. That's why I created this page as a shout-out to your efforts, whether it's teeny tiny steps or chasm-crossing leaps you're taking to include visual notes and visual thinking in your instruction or presentations. I see you. And after twenty-five years of using visuals in my classrooms around the world, I can pretty much guarantee that I've experienced any angst, excitement, frustration, wonder, laughter, and inspiration that you might be feeling as you implement these ideas.

It's worth it. That's why this page is dedicated to You. Yes, YOU. This is a yes to your story, a yes to the challenge, a yes to trusting what I'm telling you, yes to others for walking with you, yes to your beliefs. You've got this. Pass it on.

Your Syllabus

I mentioned earlier that there's no easy "hack" to visual thinking, that it does take practice and time. There is, however, one micro-hack that you can use to set expectations: create a visually-oriented syllabus for your audience.

Now I know that many of you have school or district-based requirements for your communications, especially when they go out to parents. By all means, fulfill those requirements. (Or not . . . "proceed until apprehended.") ☺ Then, on day one of your class, after students have listened to every other teacher drone on about what not to do and what grading will look like, provide your more personalized view.

If you're providing training for an organization, a visual approach to sharing learning and outcomes fights against the status quo. A visual agenda can become an immediate space for participants to draw along with you and include their own take on what is important for their particular role. It is an automatic invitation to participate visually, thus shifting engagement immediately.

We use my syllabus to talk about learning and outcomes, but it's not grade-centric. We focus on goals, thinking, and the process of learning. Students see learning as a stepping stone and that what they learn will be applied to work they do for external audiences during our time together. They will be expected to try new things, keep track of their learning, and improve upon their work with self-assessments. In other words, there's a different level of agency, presented in a very different way.

It's a definitive shift. This style of syllabus also represents my personal values for education and a desire for students to love learning for the sake of learning. Optimist, I am.

How can you use visuals to immediately invite participants to put pen to paper and become engaged in your boardrooms, classrooms, or living rooms?

YOUR SYLLABUS

Set your class apart from the others on day one with a dynamic syllabus. Bonus? It sets the expectation that sketching is a norm in this class.

Leave some parts blank so they can participate with you from the start.

WENDI PILLARS @WENDI322

Zines

Zines are little booklets that were originally created so people could share their thoughts easily to some degree. With roots in science fiction as far back as the early 1900's, they have been characterized by being self-published and no-frills, sometimes anti-authoritarian, sometimes not. Topics run the gamut. In the academic world, we have often created "zines" with our elementary students as we teach the concept of a story progression with a beginning, middle, and end, but the possibilities are endless.

Maybe there's an element of surprise or a twist, or maybe it's the first of a series...you'll find that once learners are equipped with the how-to of creating a zine, it's the perfect jumping off point for building confidence, a stepping stone for bigger ideas, and a fairly concrete way of finding a rhythm of completing something successfully. Being bite-sized, they're fun and inviting. They're also perfect for practicing small sketches, collecting sketches on a theme (i.e, animals, faces, key historical figures), exploring, experimenting and learning to love the happy accidents borne from mistakes.

To get started, imagine a topic you're interested in, know a lot about, and want others to know about. Maybe your zine will be about a collection or hobby you have, maybe it's a how-to, favorite quotes to illustrate, top 5 lists, or even your favorite activity/snacks/memes during a virus lockdown. One thing is for sure, when you create a zine it will be personal and unique with a tangible and satisfying outcome. Kids and adults of all ages can easily learn how to make one. And yes, of course, they're the perfect little place to store and sort visual vocabulary!

On the following pages, you'll find an example of a sketching zine, another that is content based, and a blank template you can use to get started with your own.

Panel 1

BOOKLET of VISUAL NOTE-TAKING GOODNESS

_____'s

Panel 2

PRACTICE YOUR EMOJIS

STUCK? COMPARE WITH FRIENDS. SHARE IDEAS! MAKE FUNNY FACES TOGETHER!

Panel 3

PRACTICE YOUR PEOPLE

LOOK at YOUR FRIENDS WHEN THEY'RE MOVING or STILL. WHERE ARE THEIR ARMS & LEGS? WHERE DO THEY BEND? WHAT ABOUT THEIR TORSO?

Panel 4

PRACTICE MORE PEOPLE

Panel 5

WHAT ARE SOME THINGS YOU LIKE? DRAW THEM WITH AS FEW LINES AS YOU CAN.

Panel 6

DRAW TWO SKETCHES FOR EACH SUBJECT AREA.

Panel 7

WRITE YOUR NAME 5 DIFFERENT WAYS.

Panel 8

DRAW A BRAIN THAT IS GETTING STRONGER AS IT LEARNS!

REMEMBER: IF YOU LEARN SOMETHING NEW, YOU WILL GO HOME WITH A DIFFERENT BRAIN!

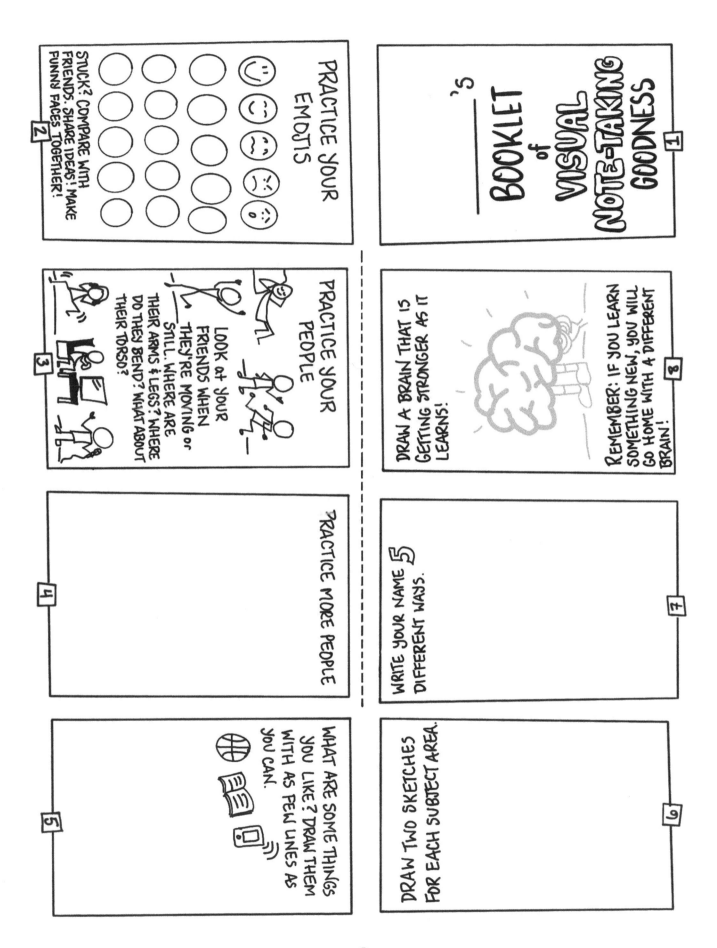

1
_____'S

BOOKLET of

ARCTIC SVALBARD

2
WHERE is the ARCTIC REGION?

EARTH ♡

The Arctic is an area of _____ surrounded by _____.

3
SVALBARD is an archipelago and is part of _____ (COUNTRY).

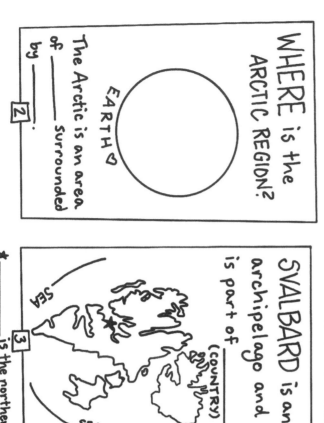

SEA

SEA

* _____ (TOWN) is the northern-most community!

4
ISBJORN is the Norwegian word for polar bear and means "_____." In Greenland, the word is TORNASSUK and means "master of helping spirits!"

5
WALRUSES are P_____ which means they are mammals that live in the sea and on land and ice. Their thick layer of BLUBBER keeps them warm in cold water; blood DIVERTS to their internal organs to keep them functioning and they turn pink!

(TRACE the walrus and draw some ice for him to be on.)

6

There are NO PENGUINS in the Arctic, but some seabirds like this Thick-billed Murre are black and white, too!

7
The Arctic is a POLAR DESERT because it gets less than ___ cm of rain and snow each year!

ARCTIC FLOWER:

In the T_____ there are no trees or tall plants because there's only a shallow active layer for roots to grow in the PERMAFROST. Plants also grow farther apart, so they can't protect each other from abrasive winds & blowing snow.

8
PERMAFROST CHALLENGE:

Can you imagine a town built on stilts? If the thawing and freezing permafrost can't support tall plants, how could it possibly support buildings & structures?

Design a house on stilts. How deep would your stilts go into the ground?

(2)

·FRONT COVER·

(3)

·BACK COVER·

(4)

(7)

(5)

(6)

Bonus Chapter:
Your Legacy and Goal-Setting 101

Ever heard of the Generation Effect? In essence, when you generate a goal in your mind, you create a picture or even a "movie in your mind." When you take the time to write that down and sketch its details, you've re-generated, or re-processed, that vivid visual in your mind, and are more likely to remember the information. That means you're more likely to keep it at the top of your consciousness and recall the details as you work your way towards accomplishment.

Quite simply, visuals (including words) have the power to transform how we think and communicate, now and for the future. After all that you've seen in this book, I'd be remiss not to highlight one of its most vital uses: to develop, track, and reflect upon your legacy.

Legacy
Legacy is that "gift" you leave behind that inspires others to do more, be more, and serve more. You are your greatest asset, so how will you show up ready to achieve and ready to conquer obstacles? Here's the secret: set your goal, visualize what you want, define and describe it in detail, and write it down. Part of the goal-setting magic is first deciding what you want to do, and just know that even if you're 99.9% sure it's something you want to do, it's not 100%. Are you ready to go all in 100%? What if you tried?

Dig in
As leaders who want to grow ourselves and lead others well, whether in our organizations, our communities, our classrooms, or our families, we have to figure out what is getting in the way of our best self. In order to do that, we need to decelerate our thinking and take some quiet time to reflect on the following:

What drives us.

What slows us down.

Our teammates.

Our solo capacity.

Our values.

Our kryptonite.

Our vision.

Our wishes.

Our wonders.

Our worries.

In my experience, both personally and professionally, very few people take the time to roll up their sleeves and truly do the work of seeing where their strengths, vision, and world's needs overlap. It's hard work. And, yeah, maybe it feels brutal. As a leader, you want to be a model, to demonstrate what you are asking others to do, to be great rather than just look great. You have much to offer, but your vision and actions need to be compelling if you're going to entice others onboard.

If you're going to leave a legacy, that is. If you're going to take life at its fullest value and go all in, then do it right. Come up with your plan and maybe a backup plan. See what kind of visualization helps spark your thinking rather than daunt it. If you're not planning on leading but simply want to level up your game in whatever you do, these words and templates are for you too, no matter your age, role, or inclination. Everyone has the capacity to improve something!

Are you the 1%?

It is said that the highest achievers, the single percentage, the one percent, are people who not only write down their goals (with detail) but review them, and maybe even rewrite them, every single day. That's crazy, isn't it? Just by writing down your goal and reviewing it consistently, you're more likely to achieve success. More likely than the sixteen percent of people who have goals and far more than the three percent who do write down their goals but without the consistent review.

What's even crazier to me is that eighty percent of the population doesn't even think about goals; I've worked with countless seventeen, eighteen, and nineteen-year olds preparing to graduate from high school who have **never set a goal for themselves**. It is heartbreaking for me, and happens far too often. It's the reason why goal-setting has become a topic I address all the time in class, amid epic eye rolls. You'll see some of the more recent templates I've created for my learners in this chapter.

Students aren't the only ones unaccustomed to setting goals, however. Adults may have short-term plans, but not necessarily life goals. Zig Ziglar, famed motivational speaker, says most people spend more time planning a vacation than they do planning their life. He also agrees that one of the most important things you can do to shape your future is to have clearly defined, written goals and a plan to achieve them. Once it's defined and written, then work on that plan each and every day. Optimize your visual thinking. Get that plan down on paper and sketch it out in detail.

Functional optimism

As you consider your plan—both the process and the outcome—you should also adopt the thinking of Admiral James Stockdale who focused on functional optimism which underpins realistic goals as well as an ability to embrace challenges, current and anticipated. There's something to be said for small wins, too, whether they be tracked as daily habits, steps, or milestones along the way, because seeing progress naturally propels humans forward. Small wins and small steps inspire a sense of hope that makes all the difference in our own engagement or the engagement of our teams as we move toward a goal.

And yes, functional optimism means rubbing those goals of yours up against reality. There will be challenges. How are you preparing to face them? As Abigail Adams penned in a letter to her husband John Adams, "These are times in which a genius would wish to live. It is not in the still calm of life that great characters are formed . . . Great necessities call out great virtues." Ask a successful leader in most any field to tell you why s/he is successful or to recount one of their greatest successes and I'm willing to bet that they'll regale you with a story about facing and/or overcoming an obstacle. So, dear Geniuses, harness that satisfaction of an obstacle soundly defeated.

Start with a guide

What follows are some templates for you to start thinking about your goals, your vision, and your own personal improvement plan, or one for your organization, classroom, family, or team. Ideally, I would sit down with you as an individual or group and craft a template geared specifically toward your processes, resources, and desired outcomes while asking clarifying questions to push your thinking. But that's not feasible here. (Let me know if you want to sit down and do that, though!) Instead, what you'll find is a variety of templates with different aspects of goal setting that I have learned about, tried, and implemented with students and adults alike. Try one template or mix and match portions of each to match or begin to build your legacy plan.

This is about you. The more you understand yourself, strengths, and kryptonite alike, the more effective leader you will become. If you take the time to write ideas down and sketch them out with detail, you already know you're exponentially more likely to achieve your desired success. It's that "simple."

This life is too short not to take advantage of what surrounds us. What's exciting—and this is infinitely cool—is that our—your!—potential is completely unknowable. Not limitless, (realistic constraints, thank you, Admiral Stockdale), but unknowable.

We do
Not
Know
What we are capable of doing, achieving, and becoming!

So why wouldn't we keep striving to learn more, do more, explore more? Why wouldn't we try to improve ourselves even 1% each day? We can all do something different, better, or more consistently by 1%. Compounded over time, that 1% will add up to monumental shifts, changes, and outcomes you never thought possible.

Just try it. Begin by writing your goal(s) down and believe they are worthwhile. If they're important to you, then they're important. Period. You're here on Earth to grow. You're here to give. Make your life count for something and do something you're proud of.

If you're still alive, you have not reached your potential. It's not about looking great, but rather about *being* great. You can do better and you can be better, so why wouldn't you strive for an extraordinary life?

May you find a spark within these pages to help you create, develop, and reflect on your life plan in both writing and pictures.

And may you live what you consider an extraordinary life.

— *Wendi*

goal-setting 101

MAKE a DECISION & WRITE IT DOWN. —JIM ROHN

⭐ FEWER THAN 1% of PEOPLE WRITE THEIR GOALS DOWN & REVIEW THEM ON a DAILY BASIS.

THESE ARE the HIGHEST ACHIEVERS.

THE MORE VIVID YOUR DESCRIPTION the MORE LIKELY YOU ARE to *accomplish* IT.

① ② I will achieve...

"GENERATION EFFECT" ×2

① GENERATE a GOAL: (CREATE a PICTURE in YOUR MIND)

② RE-GENERATE / RE-PROCESS the GOAL: (WRITE it DOWN)

EXTERNAL STORAGE → *plus* → ENCODING

"STORE" YOUR GOAL SOMEPLACE WHERE YOU WILL SEE IT EVERYDAY. (VISUAL CUES HELP WITH RECALL!)

KEEP

YOUR HIPPOCAMPUS (GREEK ORIGINS for "SEAHORSE" ANALYZES & SIFTS THROUGH INFORMATION, HELPING DETERMINE WHAT is KEPT or DISCARDED.

IF IT'S IMPORTANT TO YOU, WRITE it DOWN!

writing IMPROVES ENCODING & CHANCES FOR STORAGE & RECALL.

WENDI PILLARS @WENDI322

GOAL-SETTING

· a mini-workbook for all ages ·

This Workbook belongs to _____.

things I am GRATEFUL for ♡

MY FEARS

WHAT I will be GRATEFUL FOR IN:

AGE: ___ 2030:

AGE: ___ 2040:

AGE: ___ 2050:

1

Something I am PROUD of:

Something I ENJOY doing.

WHAT DOES SUCCESS look like FOR ME?

Success for me in SCHOOL:

Success for me AFTER I GRADUATE:

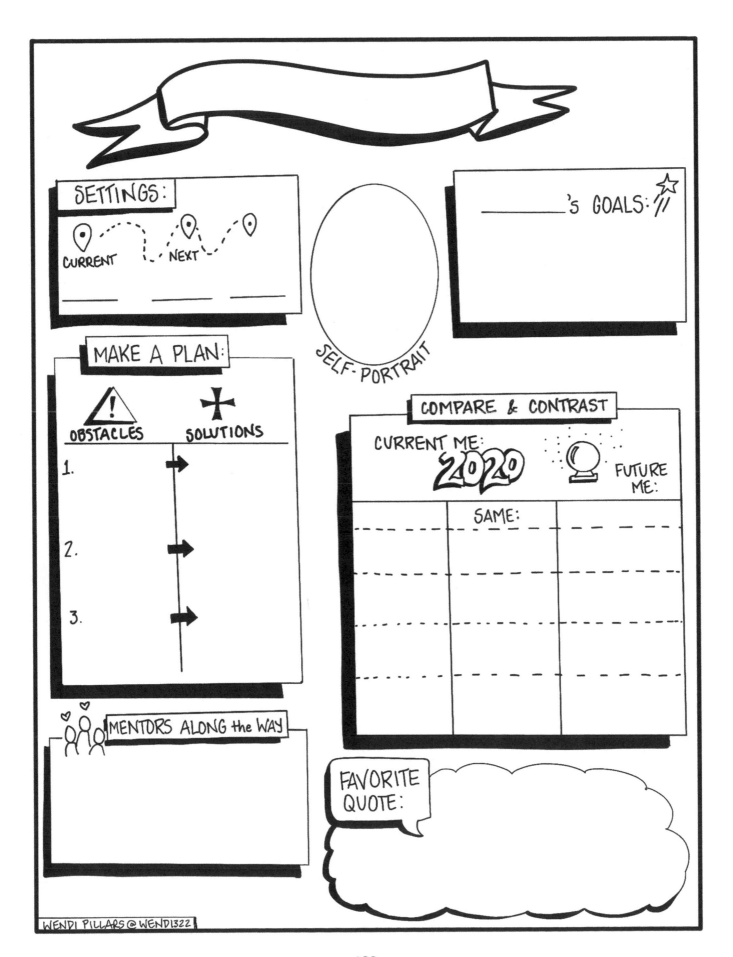

SETTINGS:

CURRENT   NEXT

_____'s GOALS:

SELF-PORTRAIT

MAKE A PLAN:

⚠ OBSTACLES   ✝ SOLUTIONS

1.

2.

3.

COMPARE & CONTRAST

CURRENT ME: 2020   FUTURE ME:

SAME:

MENTORS ALONG the WAY

FAVORITE QUOTE:

NAME: _____

INTERESTS:

NAME THREE PEOPLE WHO HAVE A POSITIVE IMPACT ON YOUR LIFE:

1. _____
2. _____
3. _____

ILLUSTRATE ONE of THEM WITH DETAIL.

3 FUTURE DREAMS:

IMAGINE THE NIGHT SKY. CONNECT A SET OF STARS TO MAKE A NEW CONSTELLATION IN YOUR HONOR. NAME IT AND WRITE ITS MYTH.

_____
_____
_____
_____

CREATE A COMIC STRIP OF A PERSONAL EXPERIENCE. DRAW ILLUSTRATIONS IN THESE FOUR BOXES. ADD SPEECH BUBBLES WITH DIALOGUE.

WENDI PILLARS @ WENDI322

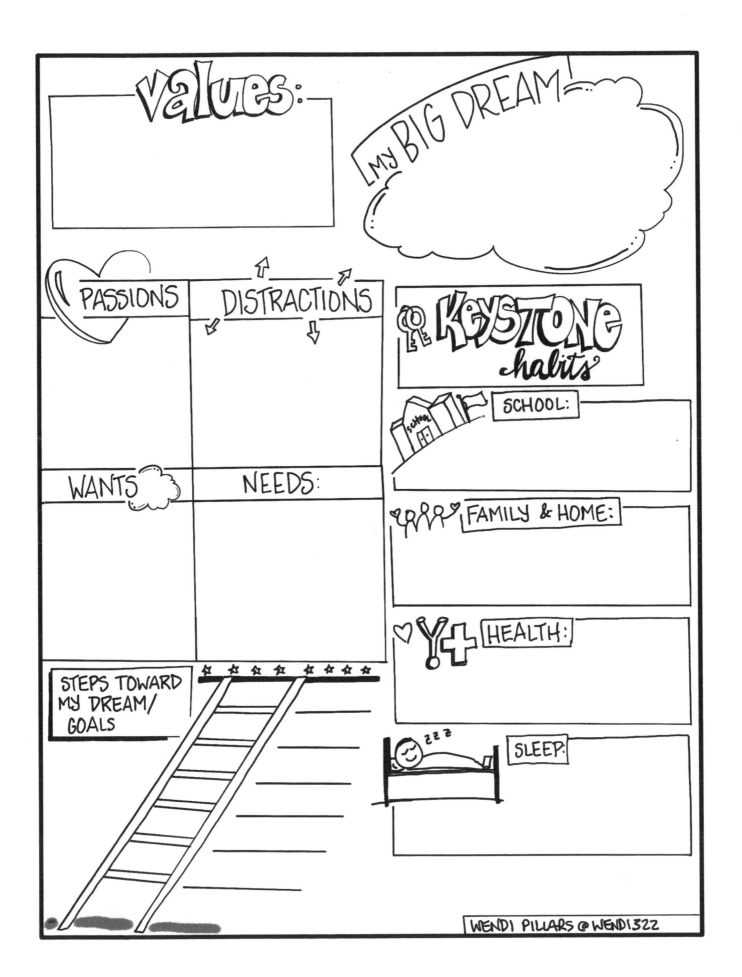

ACHIEVE your GOAL ➤ ◎

Fewer than 1% of people write their goals down and review them regularly. Those who do are far more likely to achieve their goals.

• get clear & write them down •

| START HERE | START TODAY | ADD DETAILS TO MAKE IT MORE VIVID | CELEBRATIONS & SMALL WINS ALONG the WAY |

DAY 1	
DAY 2	
DAY 3	
DAY 4	
DAY 5	
DAY 6	
DAY 7	

WENDI PILLARS @WENDI322

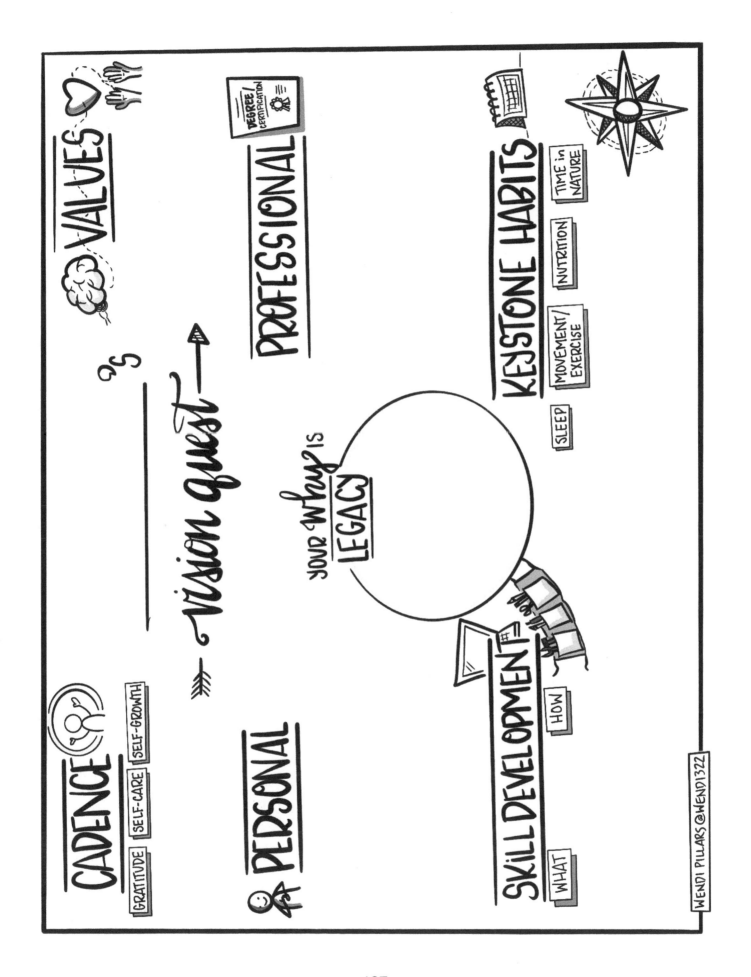

CADENCE

GRATITUDE | SELF-CARE | SELF-GROWTH

VALUES

& 5

vision quest →

PROFESSIONAL

DEGREE / CERTIFICATION

KEYSTONE HABITS

TIME in NATURE | NUTRITION | MOVEMENT/ EXERCISE | SLEEP

your "why" is LEGACY

PERSONAL

SKILL DEVELOPMENT

WHAT | HOW

WENDI PILLARS @WENDI322

—197—

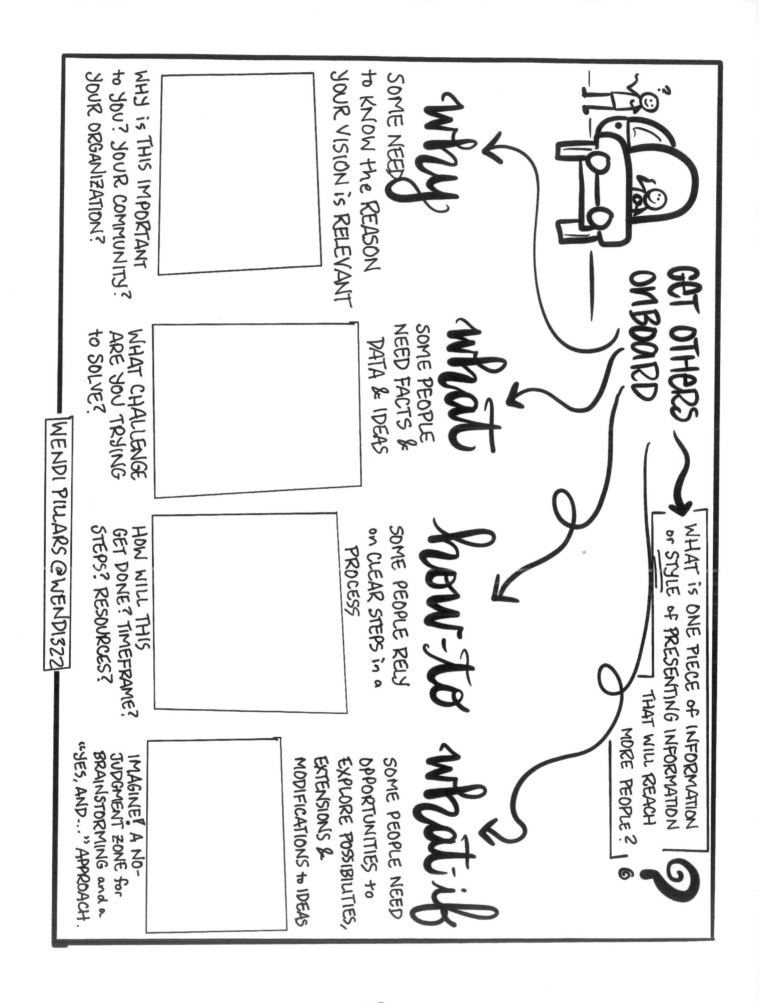

GET OTHERS ONBOARD

WHAT is ONE PIECE of INFORMATION or STYLE of PRESENTING INFORMATION THAT WILL REACH MORE PEOPLE?

why

SOME NEED to KNOW the REASON YOUR VISION is RELEVANT

WHY is THIS IMPORTANT to YOU? YOUR COMMUNITY? YOUR ORGANIZATION?

what

SOME PEOPLE NEED FACTS & DATA & IDEAS

WHAT CHALLENGE ARE YOU TRYING to SOLVE?

how-to

SOME PEOPLE RELY on CLEAR STEPS in a PROCESS

HOW WILL THIS GET DONE? TIMEFRAME? STEPS? RESOURCES?

what-if

SOME PEOPLE NEED OPPORTUNITIES to EXPLORE POSSIBILITIES, EXTENSIONS & MODIFICATIONS to IDEAS

IMAGINE! A NO-JUDGMENT ZONE for BRAINSTORMING and a "YES, AND..." APPROACH.

WENDI PILLARS @WENDI322

—198—

☆ monthly GOAL CHECK-IN

ACHIEVED ☆

MADE PROGRESS ON

GRATEFUL FOR ♡

ONE THING I CAN DO DIFFERENTLY △

RESOURCES I NEED

3 MOST IMPORTANT PRIORITIES

1. _____
2. _____
3. _____

TODAY'S DATE _____

DIGITAL DEVICE DETOX

SLEEP BETTER & CONTROL YOUR DAY w/o HAVING to be REACTIVE.

"DIGITAL SUNSET" (NO DEVICES for __ MINUTES BEFORE BED)

M	T	W	R	F	S	S

"DIGITAL SUNRISE" (NO DEVICES for __ MINUTES AFTER WAKING UP)

M	T	W	R	F	S	S

WHAT WOULD MAKE NEXT MONTH EVEN BETTER?

WHY IS THIS GOAL/PROCESS STILL IMPORTANT to ME?

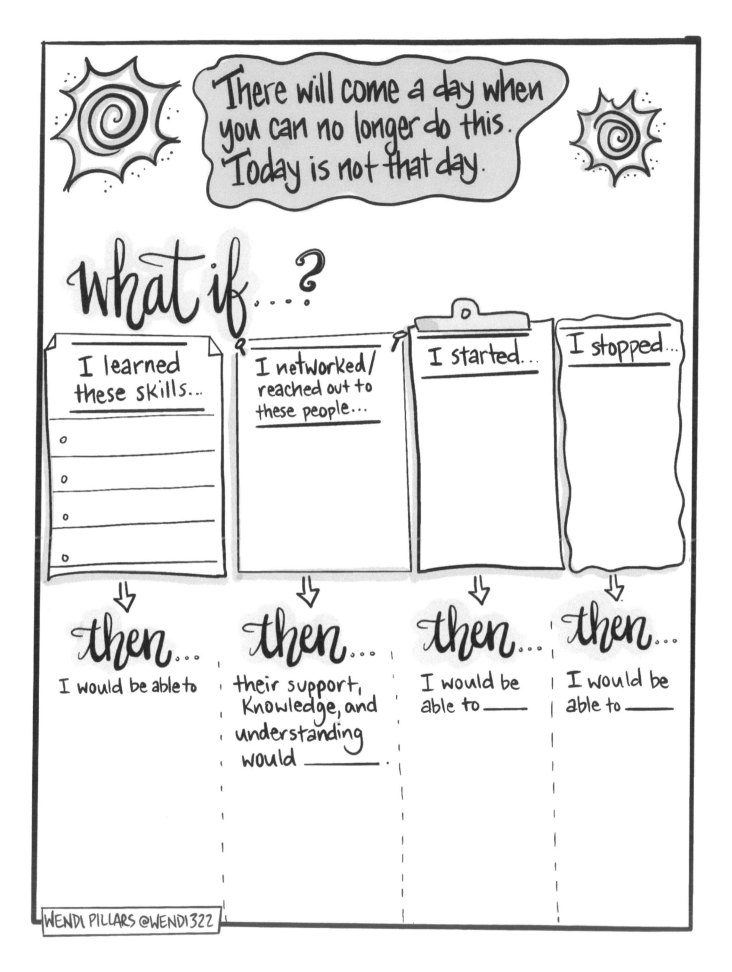

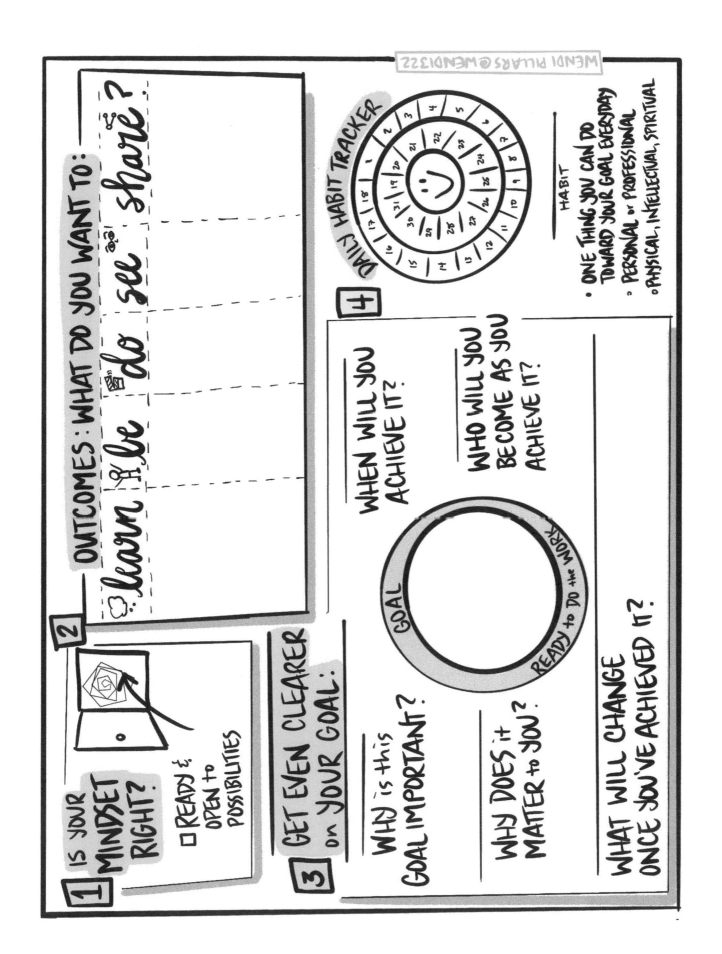

1 IS YOUR **MINDSET RIGHT?**

□ READY & OPEN TO POSSIBILITIES

2 OUTCOMES: WHAT DO YOU WANT TO:

learn & be & do & see & share?

3 GET EVEN CLEARER ON YOUR GOAL:

WHY is this GOAL IMPORTANT?

WHY DOES it MATTER to YOU?

WHAT WILL CHANGE ONCE YOU'VE ACHIEVED IT?

4

DAILY HABIT TRACKER

HABIT

- ONE THING YOU CAN DO TOWARD YOUR GOAL EVERYDAY
- PERSONAL or PROFESSIONAL
- PHYSICAL, INTELLECTUAL, SPIRITUAL

WHEN WILL YOU ACHIEVE IT?

WHO WILL YOU BECOME AS YOU ACHIEVE IT?

GOAL

READY to DO the WORK

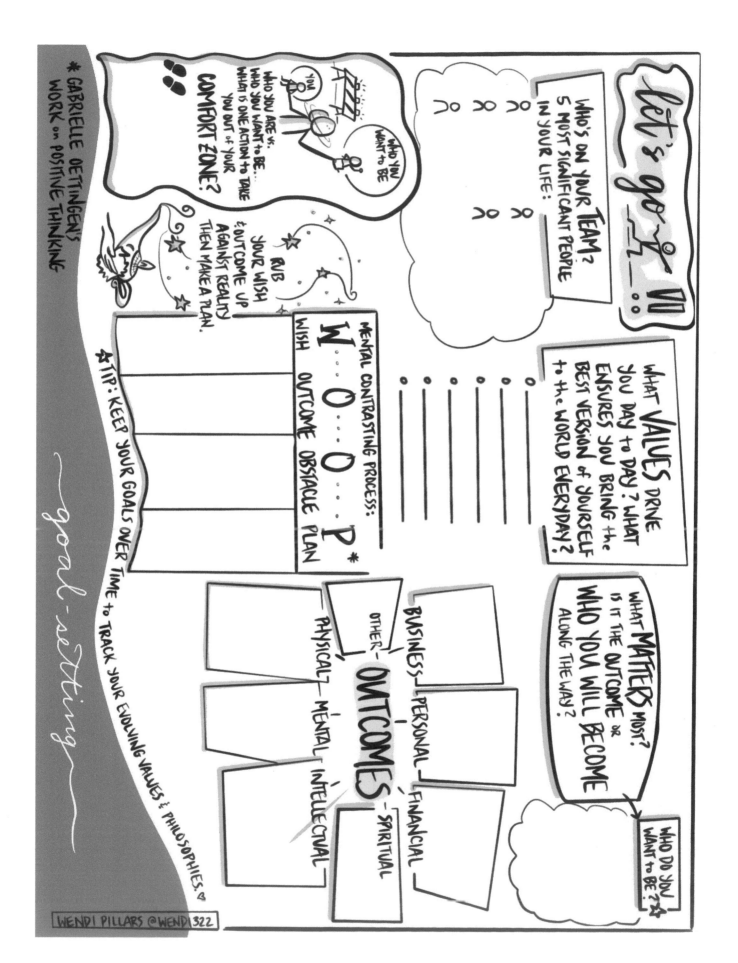

let's go ♀ VII

WHO'S ON YOUR TEAM?
5 MOST SIGNIFICANT PEOPLE
IN YOUR LIFE:

X — O X — O
X — O
X — O X — O

WHAT **VALUES** DRIVE
YOU DAY to DAY? WHAT
ENSURES YOU BRING the
BEST VERSION of YOURSELF
to the WORLD EVERYDAY?

WHO YOU ARE vs.
WHO YOU WANT to BE...
WHAT IS ONE ACTION to TAKE
YOU OUT of YOUR
COMFORT ZONE?

WHO YOU
WANT to BE

RUB
YOUR WISH
& OUTCOME UP
AGAINST REALITY
THEN MAKE A PLAN.

MENTAL CONTRASTING PROCESS:

W....O....O....P *
WISH OUTCOME OBSTACLE PLAN

WHAT **MATTERS** MOST?
IS IT THE OUTCOME or
WHO YOU WILL BECOME
ALONG THE WAY?

OUTCOMES
OTHER—
BUSINESS— PERSONAL— FINANCIAL
PHYSICAL— MENTAL— INTELLECTUAL— SPIRITUAL

WHO DO YOU
WANT to BE? ☆

* GABRIELLE OETTINGEN'S
WORK on POSITIVE THINKING

☆TIP: KEEP YOUR GOALS OVER TIME to TRACK YOUR EVOLVING VALUES & PHILOSOPHIES. ♡

goal-setting

WENDI PILLARS @WENDI322

~ let's do this ~

my VISION TODAY
+ NO JUDGMENT + EXPONENTIAL GROWTH?
+ WHAT IS TRULY POSSIBLE?

I LOVE DOING

NEED TO STOP DOING
WANT TO

WHAT IF?
...you TRIED __, DID __,
LEARNED __, CREATED __,
STARTED __, COMPLETED __, etc.

POSSIBILITIES

WHAT I NEED TO
KEEP ROCKING

TODAY

THIS WEEK

NEXT STEPS

#KEYWORD/THEME
FOR YOUR NEXT ADVENTURE.
GOAL, VISION, MONTH, YEAR, etc.

Do you use visual notetaking/visual thinking every day?

Simple answer—nope. I teach different classes throughout the day, and there are certain topics, times, and classroom dynamics that just lend themselves more readily to optimizing visual notes. Likewise, in organizations, there are certain topics and goals that similarly lend themselves to visualizing. As you've read throughout this book, there is an immense variety of ways to create the notes; take two minutes for students or participants to create a quick sketch so that you can visibly ensure understanding and where people are "at" mentally. Or maybe you're the one who creates a sketch instead of your audience, but with their input along the way. There are so many variables behind when and why I incorporate visual thinking. The best way to know what works for *you* is to jump in.

What's even more critical to understand, though as you implement visual notetaking, is that it's truly more about the thinking processes involved. This kind of notetaking makes thinking more tangible, more explicit, and dare I say, more useful? The incredible benefits derived from teams and organizations sharing the same understanding—simply because they took the time to sketch out plans while eliciting insights and ideas from each other—are unparalleled. Sending out a memo with required tasks will never have the same buy-in as grouping together to hash out ideas, harvesting thinking from partners, groups or teams, then using that same visual as a reference point as you check off milestones.

Creating visual notes also takes a different amount of time than when you talk "at" people, but in my experience the added depth of understanding and connection-making is worthwhile. I would encourage any presenter, educator, or communicator to stop and re-consider how their information can be presented more visually and with greater input and interaction from the audience. It will transform the way you approach the world.

What's your take on others copying you?

I don't mind when others copy me, at least when we're first getting started, since it might be such a new concept for them. They've got to start somewhere, and sometimes, you just have to get your own creative juices sparked. I don't, however, like when someone traces over images on their computer screens. I encourage them to take artistic license, maybe use ideas and try to draw something similar. Thinking and sketching can be cognitively taxing work, and combined with anxieties about drawing, I am really mindful about what I expect from others on an individual basis.

Have you really used sticks, stones, and dirt to create visuals?

Yes. Military after-action reviews in the field could get pretty basic, requiring the use of sticks and stones to plan next steps or recreate a mission. My experiences working in schools with dirt floors, schools with few resources, or during environmental outings are additional examples of how being resourceful ensures that learning still happens. I've traveled a bit, too, and there were plenty of times I'd want to ask questions or communicate without having a necessary level of language prowess. That's when drawings on my hands, the back of food packaging, a scrap of paper, or the reverse side of a train ticket have all been successful tools in my communication toolkit.

Is it worthwhile to sketch ahead of time for your classes?

When you create visual notes yourself in advance, you can anticipate questions learners will have and will also find yourself noticing and wondering about details you may not have noticed before. This is an important step, even if it's a very rough sketch. This goes along with pre-planning stopping points for notetaking in class, whether for quick sketches or more time-consuming ones. Doing so helps you figure out timing and gives you practice time for imagery making.

How long have you been using visual notes and visual thinking?

Twenty-five years in the classroom, but additional years and experiences have come as a traveler in foreign countries and as a freelance graphic recorder and visual facilitator with business organizations. I've used them with learners and audiences of all ages, from kindergarten to adults, both in online settings and face to face. I've used them in military and civilian worlds, in schools overseas with very few "fancy" resources, and here at home in the US with an array of resources. Please remember that the thinking piece is key. How can I get everyone on the same proverbial page? How can I ensure that everyone knows exactly what the information is about, or the tasks that lie ahead? How can I empower others to think visually and more clearly express their ideas to others?

Did you take bomb-diggety notes when you were in school?

Yes, I actually did, and I'll own that fact BUT never, not once, not ever did I doodle even a stray mark on my notes. This girl was the outline queen—remember those? I, II, III, IV, V, a, b, c, d, ... Yeah, I was the go-to whenever anyone missed class. (#nerd) I took pride in my notes, but it wasn't until I had to start communicating what I knew to others that I began relying more on visuals. In other words, it wasn't until I started teaching and trying to transcend language boundaries that I realized how second nature it was for me to dip into the visual side of thinking.

Any favorite marker tips?

For my professional graphic recording and facilitating work, I prefer Neuland markers. I like the color palettes, that they don't bleed through the paper, and the fact that they're refillable. They have different size nibs, too, so I can get really wide markers, brush markers, and chisel tips. They're also unique in that they can be used easily with left or right handers, and a little nib on the marker lets me know which way my marker nib is oriented if I need to grab a marker and write quickly.

For whiteboards, I use Pilot V-Board Master markers which are also refillable. They come in the basic colors—black, blue, red, green, and orange, with caps that pop onto the top for more ink. I try to keep a couple set aside for "me," since they're not exactly "student-proof." Students who know me do help take care of markers and know not to mash them down onto the whiteboard, but then there are those who aren't quite there with my level of marker appreciation.

For workshop participants, business organizations, and students, I rely on Crayola markers, fine black sharpies, Flair pens, and ink pens. Nothing super fancy, but they do the trick, for sure. Gel pens add some excitement to the mix, as do "guest appearances" of some of my personal stash of markers.

What's one question you hear all the time?
Oh, are you an art teacher?
Ummm, no.

Any other favorite tools for sketching?
In the classroom, I honestly work primarily with copy paper and a black flair felt-tip marker. It is not fancy, nor does it need to be, in my opinion, and works extremely well with a document camera. The black felt-tip marker shows up distinctly and clearly.

In workshops and during facilitation work, I rely on black Neulands with a couple of colors to help make the black lines pop and stand out as needed.

I do use my iPad, too, but also feel that it's unfair that I'm the only person in class with one. If students are drawing on paper, I tend to do so, as well. In business meetings, I am equally comfortable using an iPad or paper, particularly if the iPad is projected so everyone can see and use it to anchor conversations.

Oh, and my brain.☺

Anything else you'd like to share with your readers?
It's nerve-wracking to put a book out into the world and my hope is that this one has sparked ideas for you about the value of using visual notes and visual thinking. I know trying new things isn't always palatable, but this book is from the heart, from decades of experience. I fully believe that when you sketch more, you think more, and I hope you pass along the gift of thinking creatively. As a language teacher at heart, I'm pretty certain that visuals are a universal language and we would be doing a disservice to others if we didn't draw more. Thank you for exploring with me!

Final Thoughts:

I hope that this book has given you plenty of ideas of why, when, and how to use visual notes and visual thinking, whether in a boardroom, classroom, or your living room. Some ideas overlap, but you'll discover patterns to help you find a rhythm and your personal "why" for using these in your meetings, classes, and contexts the more you use these strategies.

I also hope you have seen that there are no hard rules that dictate the use of visual notes, but at the end of the day there are four general requirements I aim for. They must be:

1. Understandable—they must be legible, and visual notetakers should be able to answer clarifying or extending questions asked about them. Notes should represent deeper understanding and visual thinking.

2. Memorable—learners should know the purpose for taking this type of notes and how they are going to USE the notes to better remember the content and/or apply the information. Thinking is an ongoing process, so using notes as a tool to build upon over time will amplify the purpose.

3. Shareable—learners must be able to talk about their notes, ask different-leveled questions about others' notes, and have both pride and confidence in the work they have created. Again, this is not a one-and-done activity when the notes are used as an anchor for clearer thinking and shared insights.

4. Fun—this isn't art class, and no one is perfect. Visual notes can be a channel for fostering respectful laughter and community in a space with ideas, new learning, connections, and vulnerability—all keys to great visual thinking.

Above all, remember that visual notes are not only about content, but also serve as a window into our audience's minds. Over the years, visual notetaking has become an unexpectedly powerful relationship builder and a means of breaking down walls on an individual basis. It's not always easy, but it's brought laughter to my classes, it's made me more confident to make mistakes and be silly myself, and I believe it has made me a more attuned teacher with learners of all abilities. It's also fascinating to savor glimpses into the inner mental workings of people of all ages, whether I'm in front of an auditorium full of people or my classroom. Giving others a chance to be creative, to think and express themselves in new ways, and to consider their work with genuine curiosity rather than judgment are incredible gifts that reap untold rewards.

Thank you for reading this book and letting it spark your thinking in new ways. May you always have magic in your markers on this journey of a lifetime. Remember, when you sketch more, you think more. Here's to visuals as the ultimate universal language.

I "see" you, your confident lines, and your thinking.

- Wendi

Appendix A: Remote Supports

Sharing is vital for community development and growth. Here are just a few apps and platforms currently in use as this goes to print that you can use to encourage collaboration and support visual communication during your next meeting, brainstorm session, or instructional period.

- MURAL— shareable, shared iconography, project/problem-based collaboration ($$)

- Seesaw drawing board, with voiceover capabilities, too (free; ideal for education)

- MIRO—collaboration whiteboard with story maps, templates ($$)

- Zoom whiteboard and annotation tools for drawing

- Show Me app on iPad for recording a sketched video that you can drop into a newsletter, email, blog post, or website landing page, Google Classroom, or Canvas, etc.

- Screencastify—free Chrome extension that makes it easy to sketch with a connected iPad; can upload videos to YouTube; short time limits without ($$) subscription but super intuitive to use

- Loom—record presentations/sketching with voice over, screen recorder; desktop app or Chrome extension options; copy and paste video link anywhere

- Procreate drawing app for iPad—time lapse videos created while sketching; can then export into Adobe Video or iMovie and voice over, or simply share the time lapse on its own ($$)

- VoiceThread cloud application where individuals can upload sketches/visuals and explain them, leave comments, ask questions, and more ($$)

- FlipGrid—create a topic for others to weigh in on via short video, can show or upload sketches/visuals and comment on others' work; great for appsmashing (free; ideal for education)

- Google Slides—upload a visual template as a background image in a Google slide; insert text boxes for others to annotate directly onto the slide, ideally via tablet or Chromebook

- Inkflow app (paid and free versions) take notes, upload documents and text, and can easily resize uploaded information for annotation, movement, and cutting/pasting

WENDI PILLARS @Wendi322

LANGUAGE

BY the NUMBERS

SCIENCE

· PEDAGOGY ·

WHAT IS IT?

WHY DOES IT MATTER?

MY IDEAL ROLE

PARKING LOT

THIS WEEK'S OBJECTIVES:

ESSENTIAL QUESTION:

- o
- o
- o
- o
- o

VOCABULARY:

REMEMBER:

NAME: CLASS:

MY LIFE'S CALLING ⇒ MASTERING MY LIFE...

MY FUTURE

THINGS I'M GOOD AT

1.

2.

3.

THINGS I'M INTERESTED IN

1.

2.

3.

THINGS I DON'T MIND SPENDING TIME DOING

1.

2.

3.

WHAT DO YOU BELIEVE IS YOUR LIFE'S CALLING? WHAT CAN YOU IMAGINE YOURSELF DOING? WHAT GOALS DO YOU HAVE?

WHAT OBSTACLES DO YOU ANTICIPATE? WHAT BAD HABITS DO YOU NEED TO CHANGE?

WHAT IS THE BEST OUTCOME YOU CAN IMAGINE? HOW WILL YOU STAY MOTIVATED? WHAT WILL SUCCESS LOOK LIKE? AND HOW WILL YOU GO FURTHER?

CREATED BY WENDI PILLARS @ WENDI322

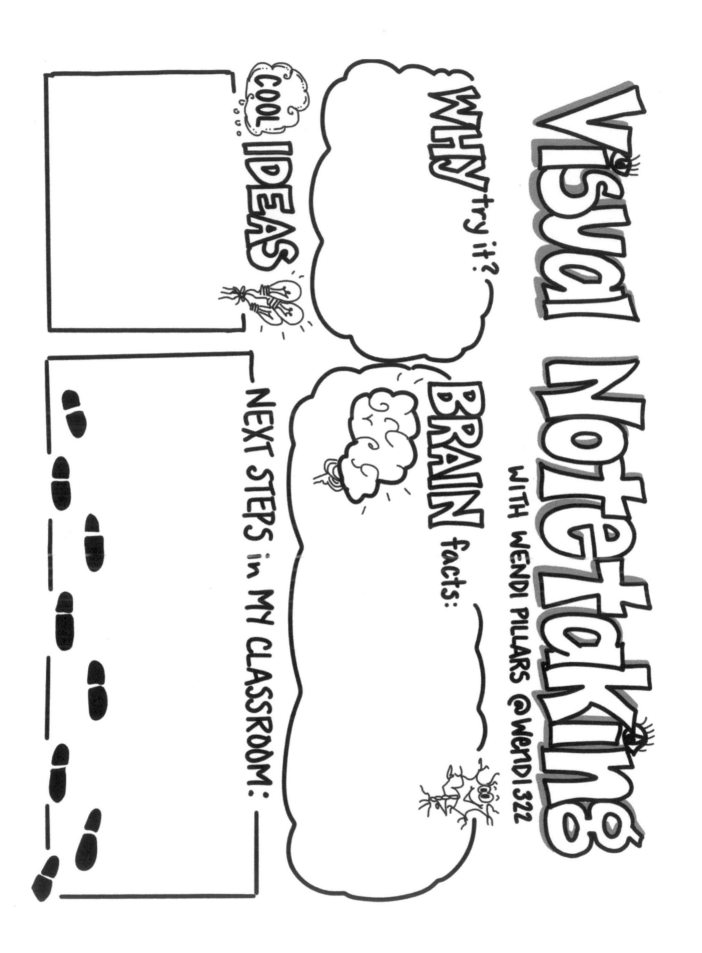

Visual Note-taking
WITH WENDI PILLARS @wendi322

WHY try it?

COOL IDEAS

BRAIN facts:

NEXT STEPS in MY CLASSROOM:

Our new vision:

Our plan to REACH, SUPPORT & GROW all STUDENTS & STAFF members.

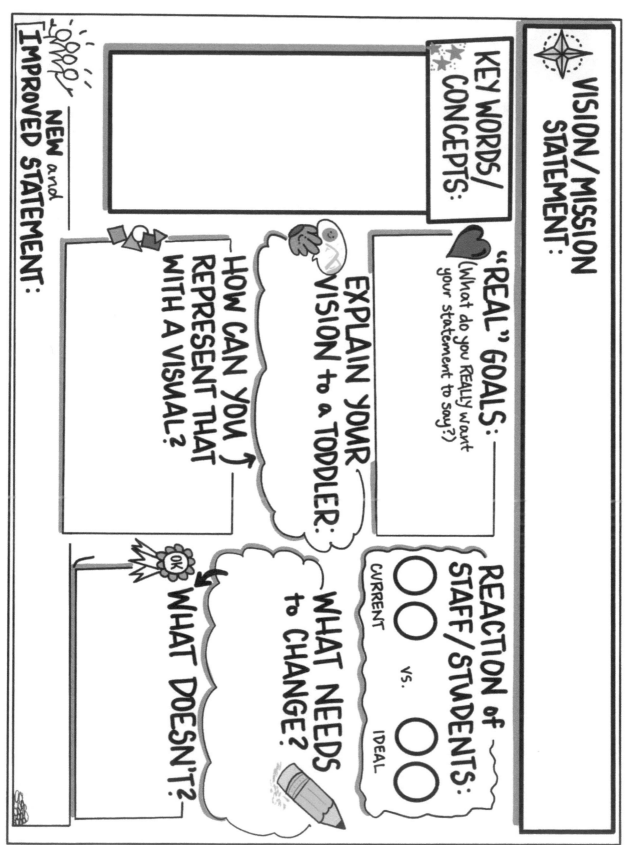

VISION/MISSION STATEMENT:

KEY WORDS/CONCEPTS:

"REAL" GOALS:
(What do you REALLY want your statement to say?)

REACTION of STAFF/STUDENTS:
CURRENT   vs.   IDEAL

EXPLAIN YOUR VISION to a TODDLER:

WHAT NEEDS to CHANGE?

HOW CAN YOU REPRESENT THAT WITH A VISUAL?

WHAT DOESN'T?

NEW and IMPROVED STATEMENT:

WENDI PILLARS @ WENDI822

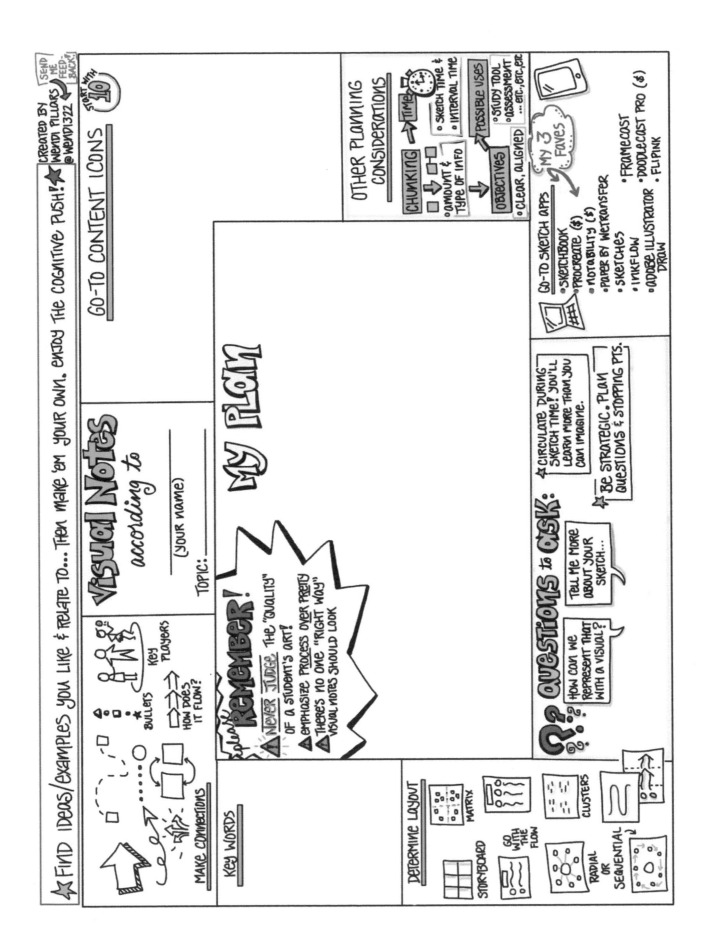

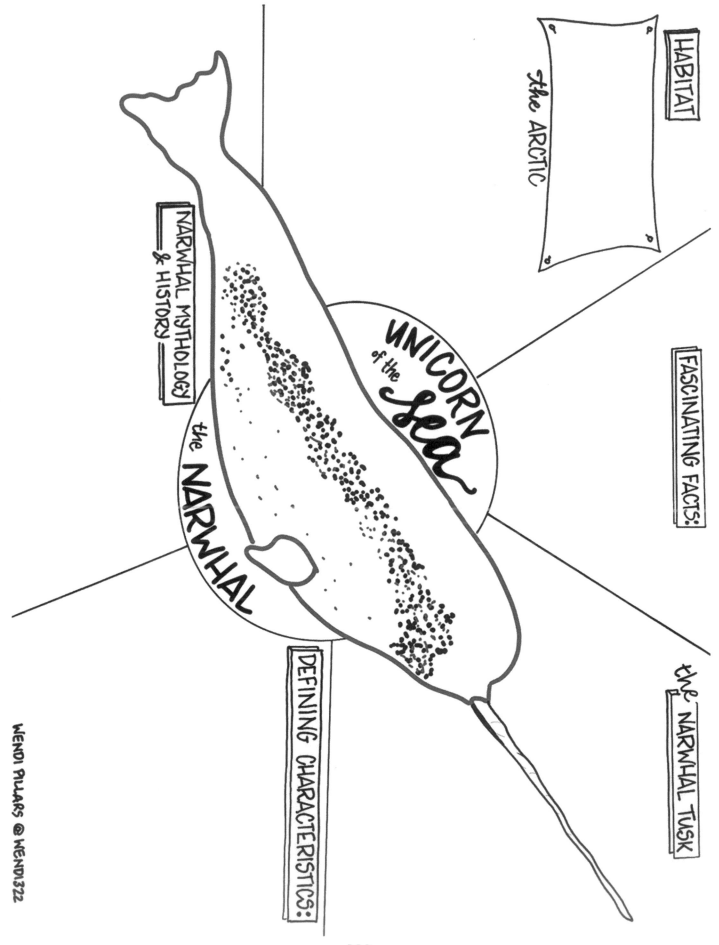

HABITAT

the ARCTIC

NARWHAL MYTHOLOGY & HISTORY

UNICORN of the Sea

FASCINATING FACTS:

the NARWHAL

the NARWHAL TUSK

DEFINING CHARACTERISTICS:

WENDI PILLARS @ WENDI322

Appendix C: Testimonials from the field

Lyanne Abreu

Lead Environmental Academy Teacher at Terra Environmental Research Institute. Find her on Instagram @lyabreuski

Visual notes have allowed my students to not only organize the information researched in a way that makes sense to their unique learning approach, but it also helps them retain the information due to the simplified context. With online learning, I wanted to adapt my teaching strategies in a way that could make learning relevant to them. To share their understanding of the material, I selected various topics they could research based on class discussions and I created a rubric with examples so they could better understand the purpose. What they came up with is better than anything I could have imagined or created myself.

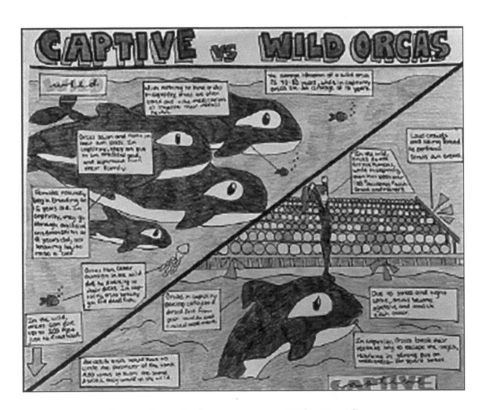

Lourdes Solorazano – 9th Grader:
Wild versus Captive Orcas. Students had to compare and contrast by giving twelve facts either visually represented or written.

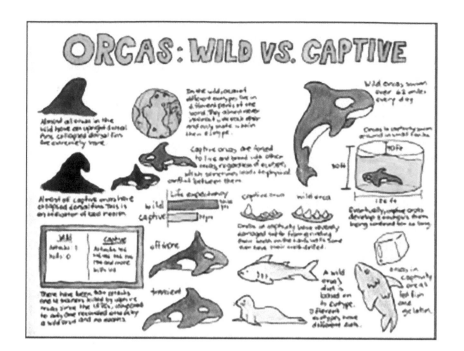

Dharma Coletti – 9th Grader

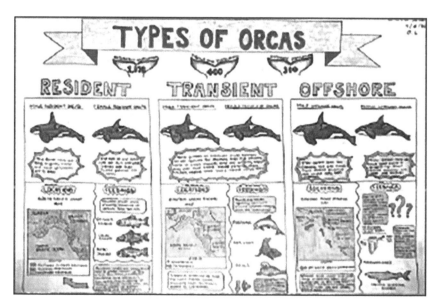

Brianna Alvarez – 9th Grader: Types of Orcas. Students had to compare and contrast the diversity of orcas in the wild. She created patterns, showing the same concepts throughout, and illustrating their differences.

Zachary Bailey – 9th Grader: Life Cycle and Behavior of Orcas had students researching what some typical orca behaviors are and how long they live for in the wild.

Elder De La Cruz, EL Instructor

Emmett O'Brien Technical High School, Ansonia CT Find him on
Instagram and Twitter @elderic22

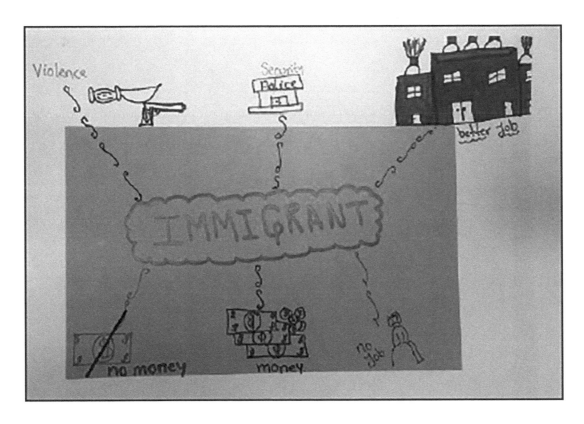

Making Predictions about a Poem

Visual notetaking is a great tool to help students make predictions about readings and to build background knowledge before reading any kind of text since it enhances thinking, language, and visual skills. For example, in this activity, EL students make predictions about the poem "Immigrants" by Pat Mora. They start the visual note by writing six words related to the word Immigrant. Students must write and sketch the words that come to their minds. The teacher can coach the students while they are brainstorming their ideas. When the students finish their visual notes, they can present them to the class as a whole or in smaller groups.

Reading and Analyzing Poems

Visual notetaking appeals to most students because it is a creative way to record ideas by using sketches, symbols, words, and phrases. It also offers teachers the opportunity to take a glance at how the students are making sense of the material they are reading.

In this activity, English Learners take visual notes while reading the poem "Immigrants" by Pat Mora. The poem can be read individually or as a whole class. Ask students to make pictures of the text in their mind as they read the poem. Students analyze and paraphrase phrases, and highlight important lines or words. Then, students make pictures of the highlighted text or words on their poems. Finally, ask the students to reread the poem, look at the image, and write down and sketch the message of the poem. Visual note-taking immerses the students in an atmosphere of creativity and engagement that leads to successful teaching and learning of the content and the language.

Tips: Teachers, do not worry about grammar or spelling mistakes when students are taking their visual notes, you will have opportunities to make corrections and provide grammar and spelling instruction later during your class. Just let your students' ideas flow. Visual notes are personal, so it is crucial to remind the students to not compare their notes with others, this is not a competition.

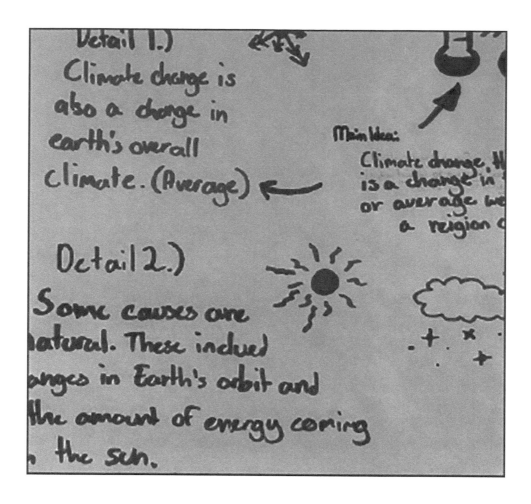

Reading and Analyzing Informational Texts

Visual notetaking is a wonderful tool that allows students to work collaboratively while reading and analyzing informational texts. Students embark on the journey of creativity while learning about facts, main ideas, and supporting details.

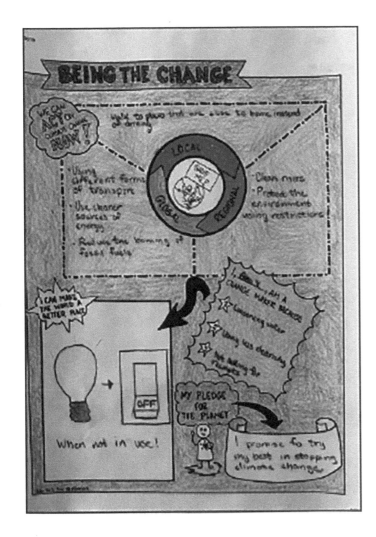
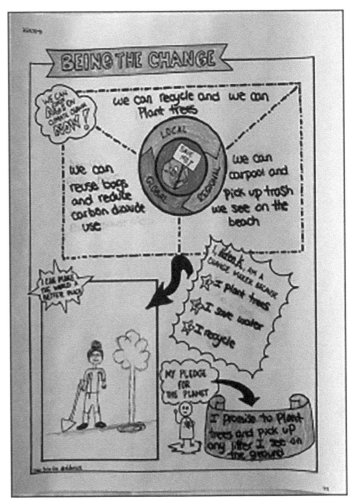

Using visual note templates is an effective technique to facilitate the use of visual notes in the classrooms. Sometimes students feel that they are not able to sketch, and by using visual templates you can offer them a first step towards making their ideas tangible. Always remind the students that visual notetaking is not about the art but about the process.

Since visual notetaking is an acquired skill, teachers and students will need time to gain experience and confidence taking visual notes, particularly at the beginning of its implementation. Therefore, it is important to provide opportunities for practicing and producing visual notes, so this practice progressively becomes more feasible. In the end, optimal learning occurs and visual notetaking makes reading and learning more fun and rewarding

DISTRICT PLAN? CLASSROOM EXPECTATIONS?

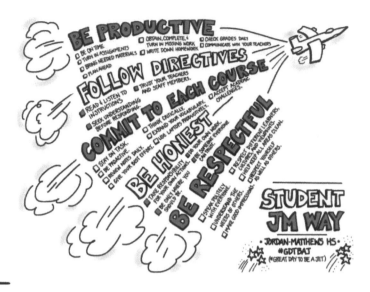

Schoolwide classroom expectations? 12-page district vision plan? Make them visual. It's far more likely they will be looked at. Plus, their one-page format makes them super easy to share in reports or on social media, either as a whole or in parts.

BLACK & WHITE

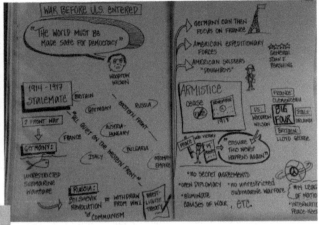

Black and white notes on notebook paper, copy paper, or recycled paper are practical and effective. Nothing fancy, but definitely personal.

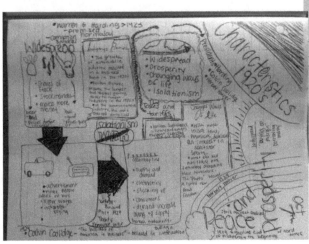

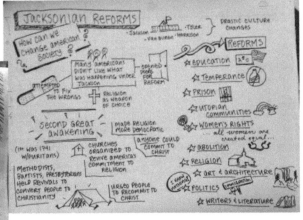

COLLABORATIVE VISUALS

Providing space for students to create collaboratively also encourages organic discussion about which information to prioritize, minimize, emphasize, and how to represent concepts visually.

Judicious use of color: red "coming from the East, representing communism".

Special thanks to Lisa Morse for her students' work.

ART ANALYSIS

Students create visuals to tell a story or represent their values around a theme. They then exchange their visuals with students from other classrooms around the world (these were from Japan) and analyze others' values. This provides an authentic audience and real engagement as the visual storyteller, while piquing curiosity as a visual analyst.

GETTING to KNOW my STUDENTS

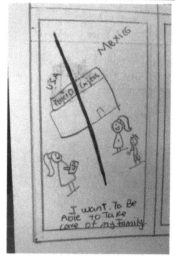

Students created comics to practice basic grammar while sharing stories of themselves as newcomers to the United States. Yes, they could have written these in paragraph format, but the imagery provides an immensely rich holistic picture of each student. Some created the images first to help them think through what they would write.

NOTE-TAKING for LEARNING PROCESSES

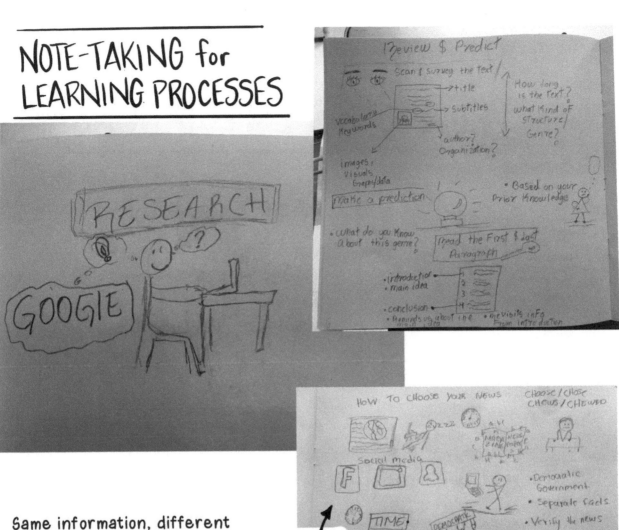

Same information, different representations/ ratios of visuals to text.

*Personalized understanding
*Immediate feedback to see what students understand and which gaps need to be addressed

CAPTURE LEARNING PROCESSES & EXPECTATIONS

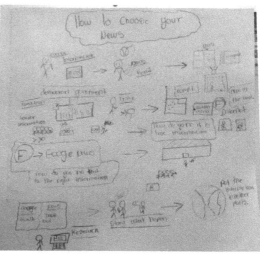

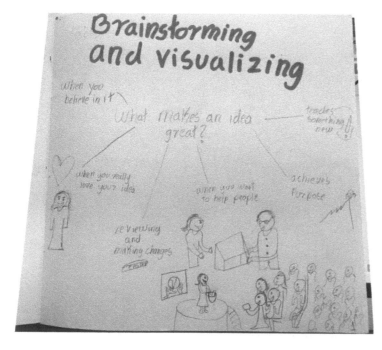

*New material
*Review material then expand upon it
* Explore connections
* Approach material from new perspective(s)
* Creating supports multiple levels of learner needs
* Learners can share and compare
* Use as a reference
* Use as a formative assessment

MARGIN NOTES
• MINI-VISUALS ALL IN ONE PLACE •

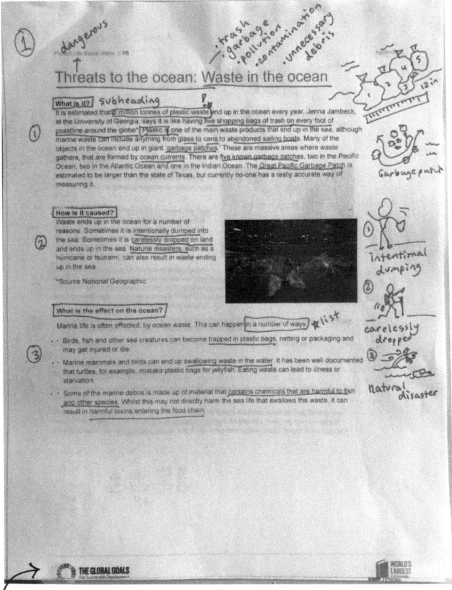

Resource: Global Goals World's Largest Lesson:
Protect Life Below Water

MAKING LEARNING PERSONAL

Retelling a story with the opportunity to add visuals according to personal experiences can provide unparalleled insights into your students.

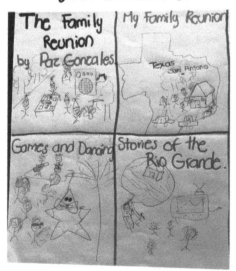

STUDENT VOICE & ACCURACY

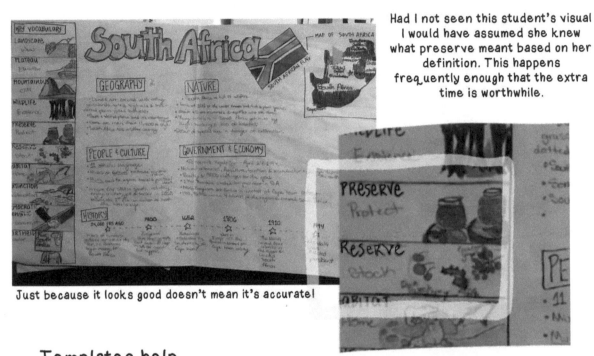

Had I not seen this student's visual I would have assumed she knew what preserve meant based on her definition. This happens frequently enough that the extra time is worthwhile.

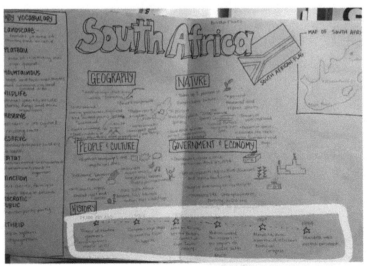

Just because it looks good doesn't mean it's accurate!

Templates help students make sense of complicated content with some structure. Just placing stars along a timeline helped students extract key events from a higher level text. Students are also free to add icons, images and color.

☆ ↑ SIMPLE VISUAL SCAFFOLDS HELP STUDENTS WHEN SIFTING THROUGH AN OVERLOAD of FACTS.

try scribing!

Have children or students unable to write yet?

Keep a calendar to remember your days. You write as they tell and draw!

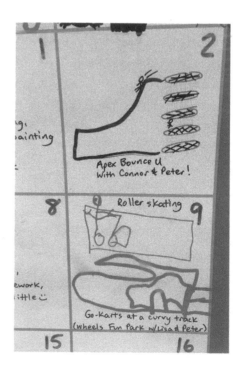

TEMPLATE VARIETY

Pre-populate a larger template with different topics and starter images around the edge. Students can then use the center space to create a visual story. This is especially useful as an introduction to a large topic or a review.

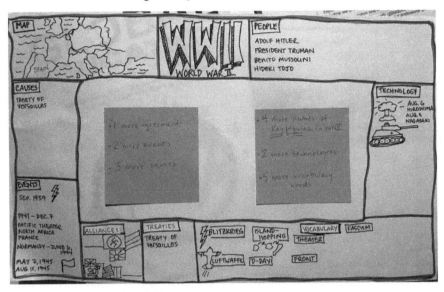

Focus on a single element of the template during a lesson or compile responses to spur discussion.

Keep it simple as a brainstorming/fact-finding tool.

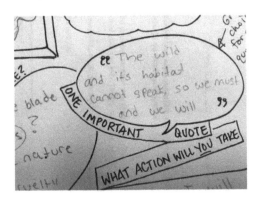

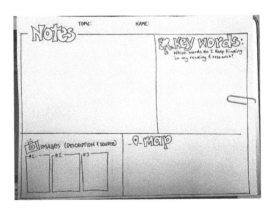

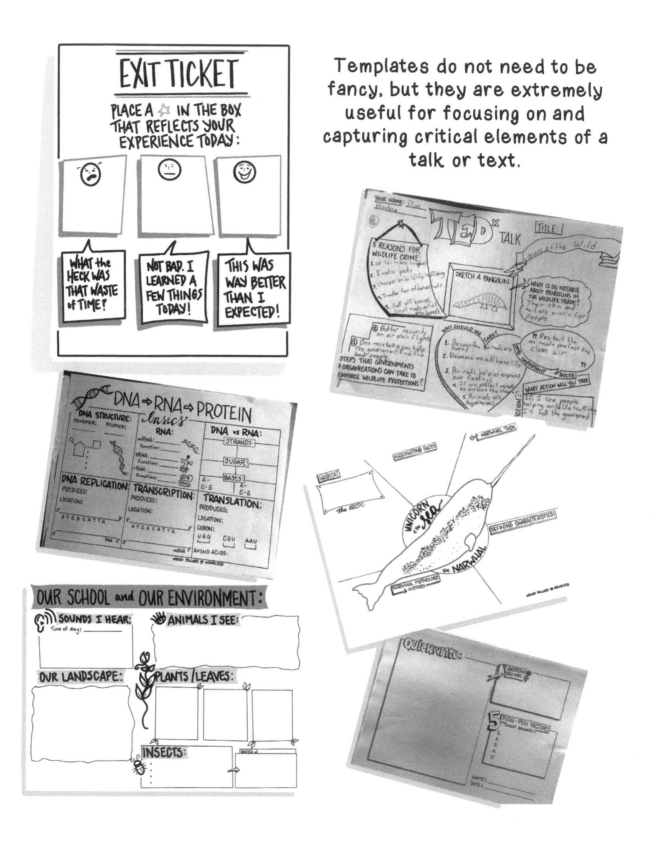

Templates do not need to be fancy, but they are extremely useful for focusing on and capturing critical elements of a talk or text.

TEMPLATES for TRANSFER

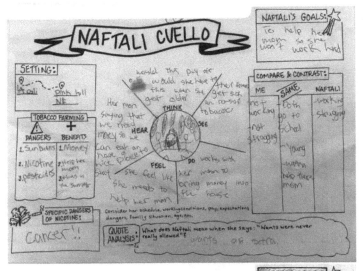

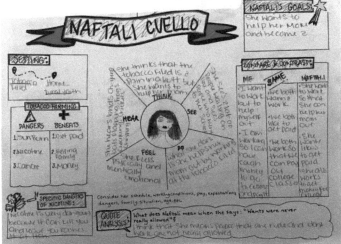

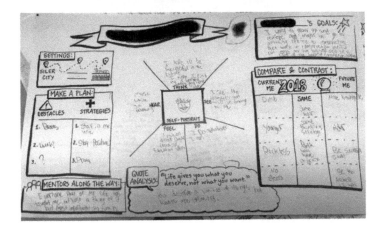

Students completed this template after reading an autobiography. They then created a nearly identical one about themselves. The familiarity with the template made it much easier for students to complete their own.

How can your templates be repurposed for additional use and prove further conceptual understanding?

NO SINGLE "RIGHT WAY"

I love to see how differently students interpret the exact same input. It's a beautiful thing that there's no single "right way" visual notes should look, No ratio of text to images allows more focus on the sense-making.

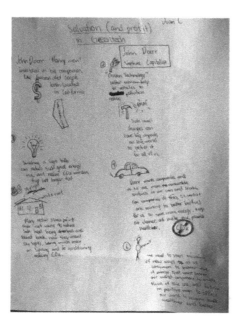

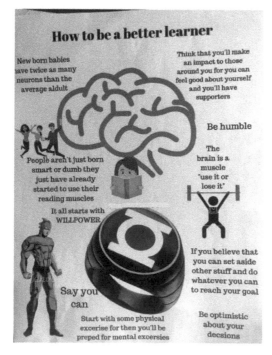

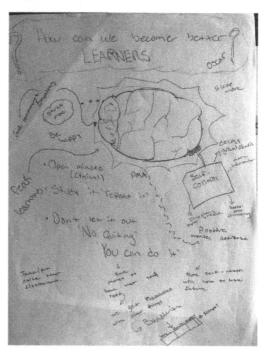

VISUALIZATION

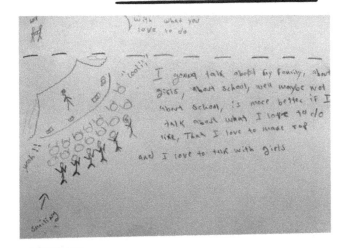

It's not enough to merely imagine success. I always push students to envision details, to draw themselves achieving their goal. I invite them to take it a step further and imagine others' reactions to their success, too. The more detail, the more likely their success. These examples were for a TED-style talk my students were preparing for.

Visuals like these are even more impactful when co-created with family members and referred to repeatedly. Think of individualized education plans (IEPs); students create and envision their goal and steps to reach it, with support, rather than just sign off on a 15 page impersonal report that ignores student agency.

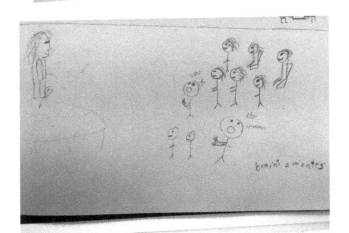

THANK YOU FEEDBACK

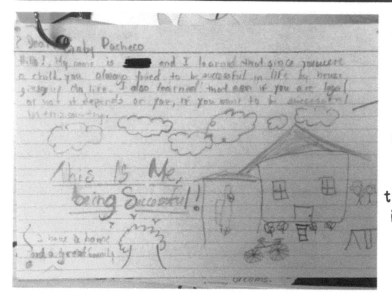

Thank you notes for guest speakers are always good practice. When students imagine themselves with clear images of their own success, it's akin to a gift.

Arete is the Greek concept of bringing the very best version of yourself to all that you do. It's a continual point of reflection for us.

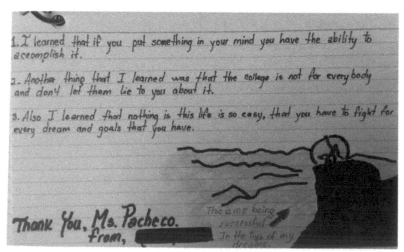

VOCABULARY

Make the abstract concrete, push thinking so that the context is clear for the given text, and invite closer observation of both the language and the content.

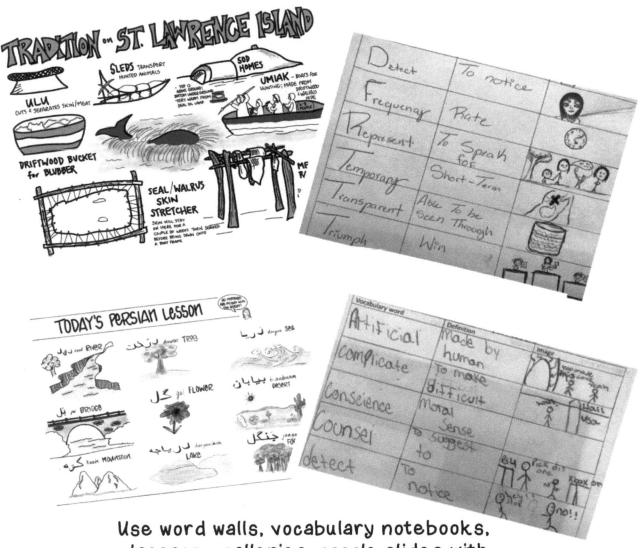

Use word walls, vocabulary notebooks, classroom galleries, google slides with classroom collections, individual word walls, and so much more.

Index

1. Hammond, Z. (2014). *Culturally responsive teaching and the brain*. Thousand Oaks, CA: Corwin Press.

2. The Noun Project. https://thenounproject.com/ (accessed April 2020)

3. Jeffrey D. Wammes, Melissa E. Meade & Myra A. Fernandes (2016) The drawing effect: Evidence for reliable and robust memory benefits in free recall, The Quarterly Journal of Experimental Psychology, 69:9, 1752-1776, DOI: 10.1080/17470218.2015.1094494

4. Zull, James. *The Art of Changing the Brain* (Sterling, VA: Stylus, 2002)

5. Crystal, David. *English as a Global Language*. (Cambridge University Press, NY, 2003)

6. Bednarz, S., Acheson, G., & Bednarz, R. "Maps and Map Learning in Social Studies." Social Education: National Council for the Social Studies, November/December 2006. https://www.socialstudies.org/system/files/publications/articles/se_700706398.pdf (accessed March 2020)

7. Grady, Denise, "The Vision Thing: Mainly in the Brain," *Discover Magazine*, June 1, 1993. https://www.discovermagazine.com/mind/the-vision-thing-mainly-in-the-brain (accessed March2020)

8. Medina, John. *Brain Rules*. (Seattle: Pear Press, 2008).

9. Weinstein, Yana. How long is short-term memory? Shorter than you might think. (April 2017) https://arc.duke.edu/how-long-short-term-memory-shorter-you-might-think (accessed January 2020)

10. Fernández, G., & Morris, R. G. M. (2018). Memory, novelty and prior knowledge. *Trends in Neurosciences*, 41(10), 654-659.

11. Tomlinson, C., Sousa, D. *The Sciences of Teaching*, Educational Leadership, vol. 77, p. 14-20. (May 2020)

12. Pillars, Wendi. *Using Picture Word Induction with beginning ELLs* http://mswendisworld.blogspot.com/2012/11/using-picture-word-induction-with.html (accessed April 2020)

13. 40,000-Year-Old Symbols Found in Caves Worldwide May Be the Earliest Written Language (March 2019). Ted Talks/ Open Culture, LLC. http://www.openculture.com/2019/03/40000-year-old-symbols-found-in-caves-worldwide-may-represent-the-earliest-written-language.html (accessed February 2020)

14. Hacha, Barbara. *Mulligan Stew*. (MediaMix Productions, LLC, 2013)

15. Dunne, Carey. November 24, 2015. *Rijksmuseum Asks Visitors to Stop Taking Photos and Start Sketching*. https://hyperallergic.com/256575/rijksmuseum-asks-visitors-to-stop-taking-photos-and-start-sketching-the-art/ (accessed April 2020).

16. Levie, W.H., Lentz, R. Effects of text illustrations: A review of research. *ECTJ* 30, 195-232 (1982). https://doi.org/10.1007/BF02765184

17. Mawhinney, J., "*45 Visual Content Marketing Statistics You Should Know in 2020*," (accessed March 2, 2020).

18. "*A Minute on the Internet in 2019.*" (Mar 29, 2019) https://www.statista.com/chart/17518/internet-use-one-minute/ (accessed April 2, 2020).

19. Gutierrez, Karla. (July 8, 2014) SHIFT's eLearning Blog, "Studies Confirm the Power of Visuals in eLearning," accessed April 19, 2020.

THE VISUAL THINKER'S manifesto

REMAIN CURIOUS at all costs. We are immersed in wonder.

mistakes are data and opportunities for *creativity*

YOUR BRAIN loves to work. Keep it *happy*

OBSERVE the world around you... And then look even *closer*.

LISTEN for the SAID and the UNSAID.

ALWAYS CARRY something to write on and something to write with.

Let NATURE inspire your thinking and feed your soul.

SAVOR the POSSIBILITIES. There truly is *magic* in your *markers*

SHARE your gifts to make the world a better place.

WENDI PILLARS @ WENDI322

Notes

Author's Note:

If you enjoyed reading this book and found a few useful takeaways or ideas to spark your thinking, please share with a friend or on social media with **#visualimpact #visualthinking**. I would especially LOVE to see examples of your work from the office, classroom, or personal use!

Readers continue to rely more on reviews, so if you could provide your feedback on Goodreads or Amazon, it would be a great help!

If you would like to contact the author, find her on Twitter @wendi322, Instagram @sketchmore_thinkmore or www.sketchmorethinkmore.com.

A Thank You:

Giving back to the community is an important part of my work and I run a dedicated mini-grant program geared specifically toward **youth** who view challenges in their community through a lens of solutions. Just as sketching out ideas makes the abstract tangible, so, too, do mini-grants bring ideas into the realm of possibility.

Our mini-grant program is called Praespero because **we are in the business of building hope and creating opportunities for hope to exist.** Once that hope exists, informed action ideally ensues, and sometimes we all simply need a boost for that critical next step. SketchMore ThinkMore will donate a percentage of all its earnings toward the mini-grant program.

Leadership, environmental awareness, empathy, budgeting, and community involvement are core values of this program, with the aim of solving challenges and fueling hope.

Mission

Our mission is to encourage students of all ages to consider their community through eyes of hope, curiosity, responsibility, and solutions-oriented thinking in order to make it a better place for all.

Vision

We want students to be curious about the world around them; responsible for other people, resources, and the environment; and empowered to make a difference as emerging or growing student leaders.

(photo by Wendi Pillars at SAV School in Bageshwari, Nepal)

about the author:

* CURIOSITARIAN, LIFEAHOLIC, MARKER ADDICT, MOM, ARMY VETERAN, LIFELONG EDUCATOR, BRAINCHANGER, MENTOR, COACH, ATHLETE, CREATOR, INTROVERT, NATURE LOVER & HOPE-TIMIST.

- Currently loving life in North Carolina with her 14-year old son, rescue cat & dog, and beloved bees.

- Author of Visual Notetaking for Educators: A Teacher's Guide to Student Creativity

- Come visit! www.SketchMoreThinkMore.com ☺

CPSIA information can be obtained
at www.ICGtesting.com
Printed in the USA
BVHW021949070921
616247BV00025B/367